The Northern Amateur Championship
at
The Moray Golf Club
1894 ~ 2005

by
JOHN McCONACHIE

Printed and Published by
MORAVIAN PRESS LTD.
31 SOUTH STREET ELGIN MORAY IV30 1LA
2005

Reproduction of photographic prints
Page 50 – courtesy of Highland Photographic, Dornoch
Page 58 – courtesy of Jack Cameron, Forres
Pages 49 and 69 – courtesy of Aberdeen Journals Ltd

For Margaret

PREFACE

THIS is a story of a championship which started in the latter part of the nineteenth century and has continued ever since – albeit under a different name – entirely due to the enthusiasm of successive Moray Golf Club Committees since 1894. The Old Course at Lossiemouth is among the top ten seaside links in Scotland and in 1992 it was given an honourable mention in Donald Steel's *Classic Golf Links*.

The history of the Northern Amateur Championship, which, at the request of the Scottish Golf Union, became the Moray Open Amateur Tournament in 1923, is little known in Morayshire or indeed at the Moray Golf Club, where it is played to this day; and scarcely at all in the rest of Scotland. This book is an attempt to set out the highlights of 100 years of enjoyable stroke and match play golf and identify some of the golfers who made it so.

A field of 111 competitors entered and played in the first Championship in 1894. The numbers have steadily increased over the intervening years, and now, in the hundredth playing in July 2005, the entries are so many that the field was closed before Christmas 2004. To accommodate the numbers on the waiting list wishing to play, the organising committee have decided to commence play in the qualifying rounds at 6 a.m. on both the Old and New courses – and so a record field of 372 players will tee-off.

Without doubt this size of field playing in an open amateur tournament must surely be unique in Scotland – and possibly in the United Kingdom.

John McConachie
Lossiemouth

CONTENTS

ACKNOWLEDGEMENTS

Firstly, I am greatly indebted to my friend Graham Kilpatrick, who has devoted a great deal of his time and energy to assisting me in numerous ways with the writing of this book. He alone is wholly responsible for the compilation of the appendix and for the mammoth task of constructing the index.

I am also grateful to such stalwarts as Farquhar Thomson, Chris Macleod, Norman Grant and many other members of the Golf Club who have given unsparingly of their time. They have refreshed my memory where it was deficient and helped to correct any errors and omissions.

My thanks are due to Bill Campbell, of Lossiemouth and Toronto, and to an old friend and colleague Dr David Hamilton, transplant surgeon and internationally known golf historian. They have both read the text throughout with their usual carefulness and offered much valuable advice.

The present Captain of the Moray Golf Club, George Reid, put his trust in me to chart an account of the Tournament years, and it is hoped that the result is worthy of his expectations. I am also greatly appreciative of my wife's continuous help and encouragement. She has repeatedly read the manuscript, and, with her eagle eye and commonsense, has spared me some embarrassment. Finally I am again indebted to Douglas Grant and Moravian Press, the printers and publishers of the book.

While researching this book, a fairly unusual event occurred. In a storeroom at the Golf Club, Graham Kilpatrick handed down a flat brown paper parcel tied with string and said, 'look at this'. On the outside was written –

> 'Presented to the Moray Golf Club by A. Low Mustard, Captain 1924. *British Golf Links* by Horace Hutchinson, 1897, No. 206 of a Limited Edition of 250 copies.

The string was unceremoniously cut with a somewhat shaky scissors and out came the large sheet edition of the famous book, accompanied by a fine picture of Old Tom Morris. The book is thought to have been there for the best part of 50 years. In spite of further searches no other such treasures have yet been found.

INTRODUCTION

I ARRIVED in Lossiemouth in summer 1973 to be the locum doctor for Dr McConachie when he and the family were on holiday. I also had a hidden agenda, namely to experience the famous Moray golf links, and my first visit was not to be delayed. On my first day the evening consultations finished at 6 pm and on the hour, the doctor's dog burst into the surgery and indicated that I should follow him. I did, and I was led to the first tee, when the dog, quite unaware that I did not have any clubs, guided me down the 1st and 2nd holes, and then cut over to the 17th tee, finally leading me up the noble 18th hole. I decided then, and still believe, that it is the best finishing hole in the world of golf. The McConachie family, all of them, were clearly devoted to golf and the doctor's four-hole habit after the evening surgery, also greatly enjoyed by the dog, explains how he kept to a low handicap for so long.

John and I kept in touch and when we both took to literary ventures later, we knew each other well enough to swap manuscripts in draft. I was the gainer from this arrangement, and John was not only patient with my erratic spelling and grammar but added crucial suggestions. On my part, since he is a natural and captivating storyteller, I had the lighter task in reading the flowing prose of his three books as they developed.

This is the story of a long-established golf tournament and is the result of meticulous reconstruction of the happenings and careful study of the participants. But the book is not just a list of worthy achievement. John McConachie has seen much change in his time, and into the story of this important annual event for the club and the town, he weaves the social changes at Lossiemouth.

Somehow he also conveys the hopes and frustrations of all of us who strive to play and win at this, the most enigmatic of games.

David Hamilton
Kilmacolm, 2005

The Northern Amateur Championship
at
The Moray Golf Club
1894 ~ 2005

HOTEL

GOLF CLUB

GOLF CLUB HOUSE

TENNIS COURT

BOWLING GREEN

VILLAGE OF STOTFIELD

LOW WATER

SANDS

HIGH WATER

DITCH

DITCH

SHELTER

No.		yds.
No. 1.	Rock,	389 yds.
" 2.	Covesea,	385 "
" 3.	Pitgaveny,	284 "
" 4.	Skerry Cliff,	480 "
" 5.	Cup,	203 "
" 6.	Table,	374 "
" 7.	Drainie,	242 "
" 8.	Gordonstoun,	350 "
" 9.	Ditch,	390 "
" 10.	St. Gerardine,	265 "
" 11.	Lighthouse,	212 "
" 12.	Target,	258 "
" 13.	V,	446 "
" 14.	Sea,	207 "
" 15.	Short,	162 "
" 16.	Road,	362 "
" 17.	Long,	512 "
" 18.	Mt. Lebanon,	387 "

Plan of the course given to Stotfield Hotel guests – 1895

CHAPTER ONE
The Moray Golf Club

The hamlets of Stotfield and Seatown were joined in the 1860s by Branderburgh to form the small town of Lossiemouth, which is situated on the North-East coast of Scotland on the shores of the Moray Firth near the town of Elgin. The inhabitants were largely dependent on their considerable fishing fleet for their livelihood and it was not until 1889 that a major change took place in the town's settled existence.

As a result of the fine springy seaside turf on land between the sand dunes thrown up by the sea, the links were seen from early days as an ideal site for playing golf. An early attempt by Elgin solicitor David Forsyth to start a golf club, to be known as the Moray Golf Club, was recorded in a minute of 2nd April 1875, and its members played on a seven-hole course laid out at Stotfield between the houses called The Camp and Skerrycliff. However, it ended in failure after some years. In 1889 – during the reign of Queen Victoria – a golf club was finally formed at Stotfield and sixteen holes, on links land closer to the Moray Firth, were constructed by the contractor, Stewart of Forres, on land leased from Captain James Brander Dunbar Brander of Pitgaveny, who was one of the founders of the club and its first patron. Within twelve months the emerging course had been enlarged to eighteen holes and golf was in full swing both summer and winter.

The founder members of the club were largely Elgin gentlemen, many of them from the professions of law, medicine and the church along with a goodly smattering of businessmen, and not surprisingly a number of well-to-do distillers. Morayshire was noted for the large number of whisky distilleries situated along the banks of the river Spey and a well-known local couplet reflected this:

> Rome was built on seven hills
> Dufftown's built on seven stills

Now, there are at least nine distilleries at Dufftown. The influence of the distiller members is still obvious in the golf club which continues to offer its members and visitors its own ten year-old single malt whisky as it has done since the foundation of the club. The present malt is *The Macallan* but this is soon to be replaced by the ten year-old single malt *Glen Moray*, an appropriate association of names with the golf club. On a lighter note, within recent memory, a hogshead of the club whisky (containing 54 Imperial gallons) was bottled on the club premises by volunteers drawn from members of the House Committee. Unfortunately this practice had to be abandoned as those engaged in the bottling process became increasingly overcome by the fumes given off by the malt whisky.

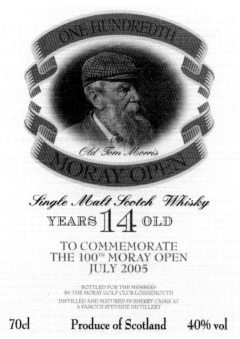

Single Malt Scotch Whisky
YEARS 14 OLD
TO COMMEMORATE
THE 100ᵗʰ MORAY OPEN
JULY 2005

BOTTLED FOR THE MEMBERS
BY THE MORAY GOLF CLUB LOSSIEMOUTH
DISTILLED AND MATURED IN SHERRY CASKS AT
A FAMOUS SPEYSIDE DISTILLERY

70cl   Produce of Scotland   40% vol

The first Captain of the golf club was the Reverend Alexander Lawson of Elgin, who, as a graduate of the universities of Heidelberg and St Andrews, had learned his golf on the Old Course at St Andrews and recognised the Lossiemouth links-land turf as similar to that on the Old Course. Old Tom Morris, the legendary professional at St Andrews, was invited to play the new course and he inspired the pioneers to go ahead with his usual encouraging words – "have nae fears, this will mak' a gran' course, or I've never seen ane". Always the diplomat, it is doubtful if Old Tom ever said anything derogatory about the layout of the many Scottish golf courses on which he was asked to advise. But on this occasion I think he meant it.

An unusual action photograph of Tom Morris circa 1890

The success of the new club – named The Moray Golf Club at Lossiemouth – was immediate, and, although it continued to be composed largely of Elgin gentlemen, it attracted members from all over Scotland. Soon its fame was such that English and London gentlemen and their ladies, visiting in the summer months, applied for membership in considerable numbers. Large numbers of English visitors had been coming to Lossiemouth for the months of August and September since the advent of the railway in 1852 and by 1904 the popularity of Lossiemouth and its celebrated golf course was such that the visitors had increased the membership to over 500 and, significantly, 135 were lady members.

The Stotfield Villas

Today that prosperous era for the golf club is still marked by the large houses and villas at Stotfield which were built by the wealthier visitors as their summer residences. In that category were Mrs Willock-Pollen and her husband H.C. Willock-Pollen, Lord of the Manor of Little Bookham in Surrey, who arrived in their chauffeur-driven car each summer to spend a month or two in their large dwelling house at Stotfield. The house is still aptly known as 'Firthside' from its position perched above the shoreline of the Moray Firth with its sweeping views of the Caithness and Sutherland coasts to the north and west. The main row of Stotfield houses overlooks the 18th and 2nd holes of the Old Course and forms a natural amphitheatre. The Stevenson lighthouse at Covesea is a prominent landmark at the far end of the links and was immortalised by club member David West R.S.W., noted artist and scratch golfer, on the cover of the famous Players cigarette packet. The fine sandy beach, with its dressing boxes and bathing as safe as anywhere in Scotland, was another notable feature.

The Stotfield Villas lining the 18th and 2nd fairways

What were the attractions of Lossiemouth in those far distant days? The sun which set in January in the south-west, set in midsummer almost in the north. Long lazy afternoons, warmed by the Gulf Stream as it flowed around the north of Scotland and down into the Moray Firth, merged into long evenings where the light permitted play on the links until almost eleven o'clock at night. The climate was milder than that of St Andrews

4

The fourth Skerrycliff green in 1893 with a well dressed caddie in attendance

and North Berwick, more bracing than Nairn, and one of the driest in Scotland, with an average rainfall of less than 21 inches. Such a beautiful setting for a golf course ensured the popularity of the Lossiemouth links and its place in the fewer than 400 courses in Britain at that time, was a high one.

An Unusual Strike

As the membership continued to grow, problems arose and newspaper reports of the time suggested some tensions between the male and female members. These ladies were not timid – many of them were members of London society and wealthy in their own right – and they took exception to the perceived dominance of the male golfers which was enshrined in a rule which stated that men had to be allowed to play through in all circumstances.

By 1905 the Council was aware that something had to be done to pacify the lady members and relieve the congestion on the links, and a new Ladies/Relief course of nine holes was built within the existing 18 hole course. In the summer months a starting sheet was in operation from 9am until 6pm and a full-time starter was in attendance in his little box on the first tee. The members of the Council were anxious to avoid reviving a situation which had arisen in 1902 and had attracted some unwelcome publicity for the Moray Golf Club – particularly in the London area. On March 27th 1902 a report in the magazine *Golfing*, which was published in London, had attracted a good deal of attention, and not a little mirth, in the golfing world. The following is an extract from the article.

> A rather curious strike is reported from Morayshire. The ladies of the Moray Club have 'struck' against the gentlemen and eighteen of them have resigned. The quarrel, it seems, is all about a window. The ladies wanted an additional window in their sitting-room in the clubhouse. Their lords and masters of the committee declined to do the work on the ground of the club's poverty. A Bazaar was then proposed to put in funds, and the ladies worked with such heartiness for the success of the Bazaar that no less than £1000 was netted.

> They then repeated their application, thinking that there would no longer be any difficulty about providing the new window. But the committee still declined on the ground that the club's finances did not warrant it. So eighteen ladies sent in their resignations, and now, as the local paper says, it has come to be a question of losing the ladies or making a window.

This put the Council in a fix. The full story was that when the second clubhouse was built (utilising the original stone building constructed and opened in 1892), a grand Bazaar to raise funds had been held in the Town Hall, Elgin on the 8th, 9th and 10th August 1901. The ladies had put a great deal of effort and hard work into the venture which had been opened on successive days by three prominent club members – Dr A. M. Fairbairn, the first Principal of Mansefield College, Oxford, Colonel Sir George Cooper of The College, Elgin, and Colonel Sir Felix Mackenzie of Forres.

This Bazaar had raised £997:7/- and covered a large part of the costs of the new clubhouse. The ladies' second Bazaar had raised £1000, all for a new window - in truth it was to enlarge an existing small window in their locker room. What the Council had done was to expropriate the money and regard it as part of the club's general income. The outcome was never in doubt. The Council caved in, the ladies were granted their enlarged window, and the club profited financially.

Overseas Members

The club enjoyed a large number of Scottish overseas members from every quarter of the globe when the British Empire was in its heyday and they are commemorated today by the handsome Jacobean clock they left in the clubhouse with its somewhat emotive verses from the pen of 'H.B.' of the humorous magazine *Punch* – who was himself an overseas member.

Presented by the Overseas Members to The Moray Golf Club – 1927

By distant rough, lone bunkers, far-flung tees,
Man's laboured rounds the eighteenth green attain,
So we, the leave men of the Seven Seas,
By devious routes this common harbour gain.

And here we set this tallyman of time,
Bidding him mark our minutes disappear
Less slowly in the far and alien clime,
Less swiftly – oh! less swiftly – when we're here.

Northern Amateur Golf Championship Meeting

AND HANDICAP COMPETITION

ON THE

LINKS OF THE MORAY GOLF CLUB, LOSSIEMOUTH,

ON

Tuesday, Wednesday, and Thursday, 3rd, 4th, and 5th September, 1907.

Regulations for Competition.

1. The Competition will be open to Members of all recognised Golf Clubs.

2. Competitors must lodge their Names and Addresses with Mr. A F. MACDONALD, Solicitor, Elgin, the Honorary Secretary of the Moray Golf Club, on or before WEDNESDAY, 28th August, together with Entry Money and a note of their Club's Handicap, certified by the Secretary of their Club ; also, the Scratch Score of their Green. The Entry Money will be—For Members of the Moray Golf Club, 5s ; and for Non-Members, 10s.

3. Two Rounds of the Course (Medal Play) will be played on 3rd September for Six Handicap Prizes, the Lowest Aggregates, after deducting Handicaps, to win. The Handicap Prizes will be of the following values :—£5 5s, £4 4s, £3 3s, £2 2s, £1 11s 6d, and £1 1s.

4. On 4th September the Sixteen Players with the Lowest Aggregate Scratch Scores of the previous day shall play by Holes for the Trophy known as the Moray Golf Club Trophy (value £50;. The first and second rounds will be played on the 4th, and the semi-final and final on the 5th September. Unsuccessful competitors on the 3rd September, excepting members of the Sixteen, will compete on the following day, under handicap, for Two Prizes of the value of £2 2s and £1 1s. One Round of the Course (Medal Play) will decide the winners. The Draw and Hours of Start will be fixed by the Committee and posted at the Club-House.

5. In the case of ties for the Handicap Prizes or for a place in the Sixteen the Competitors will immediately on the result being posted at the Club-House, play on until one has a lower score than the other, unless otherwise directed by the Committee, who may decide ties otherwise if they see fit. Any Competitor not ready to start as above provided for will lose the tie. In the event of ties on the 4th and 5th in any of the first Three Rounds (Match Play) the Competitors tieing shall play on until one of them wins a hole, when he will pass into the next round. In the event of a tie in the Final, it will be decided by a full round.

6. The Winner of the Hole Competition shall be the Northern Champion (Amateur) Golfer for the year, and the Trophy shall be held for that year by the Club from which the Winner shall have entered, but shall remain the property of the Moray Golf Club, to whose Secretary it shall be returned by the first day of August in the following year. The Winner and Runner-up shall each receive a Gold Medal.

7. Play will commence on the 3rd at Nine o'clock A.M.

8. The handicapping shall be under the control of the Council of the Moray Golf Club, and the Competition will be played in accordance with the Rules of that Club.

9. The result of Ballot for Partners, Handicap, and Order of Starting on the 3rd will be posted to each Competitor.

10. Competitors will be made Honorary Members of the Moray Golf Club for the week ending 7th September.

11. The Council of the Moray Golf Club reserve power to reject any entry without assigning any reason therefor, and to alter or amend any of the foregoing Rules or Conditions, and all disputes shall be finally decided by them.

By Order of the Council of the Moray Golf Club,

A. F. MACDONALD, *Hon. Secretary.*

CHAPTER TWO
The Northern Amateur Championship

The first national Amateur Championship in Britain was organised by a group of enthusiastic gentlemen amateurs from the Royal Liverpool Golf Club at Hoylake. It was played at Hoylake in 1885 and won by a Scotsman, A. F. Macfie of the Royal and Ancient Golf Club at St Andrews, who, at the 14th hole in the fourth round, had the first hole in one at the Amateur. Allan Fullarton Macfie was said to be the most assiduous and scientific of practisers and when the caddies appeared at Hoylake in the morning and found the links scattered with balls they always knew that Macfie had been out the night before.

In David Hamilton's definitive history of golf, published in 1998, he describes this as the era of gentlemen amateurs and notes that the planners of the event had some difficulty in keeping the Championship an open event, yet closed to undesirables. The Liverpool captain stated that it was not in the interests of golf if 'a valuable prize [ie the Amateur Championship] was won by a fisherman or a weaver from Scotland'. There is no evidence that the weavers and fishermen wished to join the gentlemen's play, but obstacles were erected. The entrant had to be an amateur member from a recognised golf club, there was to be a high entry fee and there would be no prize money which could be used as travel expenses. It was arranged that the format would be a week-long match-play marathon outside the usual holiday time and such an event would be difficult to attend by ordinary wage-earning players.

The list of entrants for the Amateur Championship shows that they came from the blue-blooded clubs only. In the 1886 Amateur Championship at St Andrews there were 42 entrants of whom 25 were from St Andrews and all of these were from R & A members, in spite of the presence of other flourishing clubs in the town. Two entrants were disqualified because of having at one time 'carried clubs' and no doubt these were talented local players*

Golf – Scotland's Game by David Hamilton at the Partick Press (1998)

The 2nd tee at St Andrews in the 1890s – Leslie Balfour-Melville on the tee

Captain Ladds driving from 1st tee at Moray in 1893.
Greenkeeping as sophisticated as St Andrews.

The Moray Event

Conditions in Scotland (which had introduced the game to the world) provided a rather different background into which The Northern Amateur Championship at Lossiemouth was first launched in 1894, but it has to be said that the idea of the gentleman amateur was still in evidence among some of the summer visitors. This Championship, which is now played as the Moray Open Amateur Tournament, is one of the oldest amateur tournaments in the world. The responsibility for this first Championship lay with the fifth captain, W Monro MacBey, the Elgin land surveyor who drew up the plans, which hang in the clubhouse today, for the original 16 hole course at Stotfield. By contrast the first (unofficial) Open Championship of America was played in the same year of 1894 and four players took part. The first Scottish Amateur Championship was inaugurated in 1922, almost 30 years after the Northern Amateur at Lossiemouth.

From the outset the Northern Amateur was a great success and attracted 111 entries – more than the 64 entries for the British Amateur Championship of 1894 which was again played at Hoylake and won by the great gentleman amateur John Ball of Royal Liverpool. John Ball was one of the finest amateur golfers of all time winning the British Amateur eight times and in 1890 being the first amateur golfer to win The Open. He played his last Amateur at the age of 61 and said to a friend in the clubhouse after being beaten in the sixth round, 'if only a storm would sweep across the links from the Welsh hills I feel I could beat all of them once again'.

After the successful conclusion of the first Northern Amateur glowing accounts of the golfers and their successes appeared the following week in the *Elgin Courant* and the *Lossiemouth Bulger. The Bulger* was published twice monthly and advertised itself as *A Summer Journal for Lossiemouth, Elgin and Neighbourhood – Price One Penny.* This edition carried nature articles, poetry, a leader on the proposed appointment of a Professor of Divinity in Aberdeen and of course, as it was named after the wooden golf club of that time, a splendid account of a great day of golf.

It is clear that the Council were surprised by the success of their Championship. The competitors on Saturday 25th August 1894 included a fair number of scratch golfers and the scores were good when the conditions of play were taken into account. Greenkeeping was less than sophisticated with sandy stretches interrupting the fairways. The whins were in places impenetrable and the teeing grounds and bumpy greens left much to be desired. Bunkers were but irregular breaks in the links moulded by the wind, rain and burrowing animals. With the gutta percha ball and the scare-neck wooden clubs liable to break, a round of 18 holes could turn out to be a hazardous event – without taking account of windy weather. Play was over 36 holes in this Championship and with lunch this took only five hours.

At the end of a long day of great excitement, both for the competitors and the large number of eager spectators, the result was declared. Three players were tied on 170 – John Sutherland, the Dornoch secretary, J.H. Andrew of Prestwick and L.W. Macpherson, an Edinburgh medical student playing out of Baberton. After a play-off over nine holes, Andrew was declared the winner and late in the evening the handsome trophy was presented to him by the donor William Christie Snr. of the Station Hotel, Elgin. Even later in the evening Andrew had to hand the trophy back as it was discovered that on one hole his partner had putted first and knocked Andrew's ball into the hole.

The club secretary contacted the R&A at St Andrews by telephone and an official ruled that Andrew was disqualified as he should have replaced his ball and then holed out, thereby adding another stroke to his score. A second play-off was ordered on the following day and L.W. Macpherson was finally declared the winner. Macpherson played out of Muswell Hill in London after he graduated in medicine and he was runner-up over 72 holes in the following year and winner again in 1897 and 1898. Under the rules he then took possession of the trophy and the club commissioned the London silversmiths Mappin & Webb to make the present handsome trophy at a cost of a little over £39. Today this cup is valued at over £12,000 and prudently no longer leaves the club. Dr Macpherson's widow returned the original trophy to the club and it is now awarded to the winner of the low handicap section.

The Bulger

The leading article in The Bulger on the following Wednesday waxed lyrical about the Championship.

A Summer journal for LOSSIEMOUTH, ELGIN, and NEIGH-BOURHOOD

LOSSIEMOUTH, WEDNESDAY, AUGUST 22, 1894.

From the rising to the setting of last Saturday's sun, Lossiemouth at its west end was *en fete*. Shortly after eight the "knights of the cleek" who were early risers began to gather at the golf house, and this early bustle, with the May-day tents on the green, told the passer-by who had not read his Bulger that the Moray Golf Club was beginning a day of exceptional interest. As the morning wore on, the crowd of visitors and players increased, and the flaring red of the golfer's jacket, which predominated the earlier hours, was swallowed up in the parasols and attire of a well-dressed holiday gathering. The golf fever had seized the town. Polite people were whispering the surnames of the champion players, as we have heard a grand stand bevy on Epsom Downs utter the name of the favourite on Derby Day: and those who have never handled a cleek nor read a line of any of the literary saints of the game, demanded scores and buried themselves with "spy-glasses".

Up until the morning of the game – thanks to the Club Committee and the fame of the course – everything had gone like clockwork. Golfers came from Dan to Beersheba of the world's links and the usual *esprit de corps* of the golfing enthusiast had provided good excuses for long journeys and the moral risks of a whole day's golf playing. We had a preliminary survey of the spoils of the toornay, and for once in our life the "pot-hunting" spirit came upon us and our palms itched to grasp a driver. We were never in such humour to shout "fore". But we had memories of the sandy wastes of Sandwich (we like the Bell Hotel better than putting greens), the forest glades of Chingford, the heathy stretches of Woking, the farmer's field of Richmond, and the grassy slopes of Southampton – and in all we wrestle with the ball too strenuously, so we lit our pipes and went out to look at the morning. By half-past eight in the morning everything was ready for a start and it was decided to begin. A clump of players, attended by their ragged and barefoot squires, the caddies, stood in front of the secretary's tent. There was one man there the centre of a circle. He surveyed the course like a longshoreman; talked with his chin on his chest and a drawl of knowledge in his voice. He was a scratch of reputation and already armed with his bulger.

There was much more in the same vein with long accounts of how the scratch players made their scores. The newspaper took its name from a wooden club with a convex face designed by Robert Simpson, one of six well-known golfing brothers from Elie in Fife. Robert had a substantial workshop in Carnoustie where he employed up to 25 men, and he made the 'bulger' to the design of Henry Lamb who was beaten by Horace Hutchinson in the Amateur Championship of 1886 at St Andrews. The club was made with a yellow thorn head four inches in length.[*]

Garden G. Smith was an Aberdonian and a golfer of some note at Royal Aberdeen who gave his home course as North Berwick. Smith had played in the British Amateur at Hoylake in April and had been beaten by that fine golfer Leslie Balfour-Melville. Smith had sent in his entry for the Lossiemouth Championship but was unable to play in the qualifying rounds because of a bad cold. He was for many years editor of *Golf Illustrated* and the account of the play in *The Bulger* seems to bear the stamp of his writing.

The second Championship was won by A.J.T. Allan, a 20-year old medical student from Edinburgh. Allan had been playing golf for only

[*]Golf in The Making by Henderson & Stirk Ltd. 1979

three years but had already broken the course record for the Braids course at Edinburgh with a 69. He played in his walking shoes and beat his fellow medical student Macpherson into second place. He then qualified as a doctor and won the British Amateur Championship in May 1897 at Muirfield. He died the following year at the early age of 22. His name is commemorated in the present day by the 'Jack Allan Trophy' which is presented each year to the winner of the Scottish Universities individual championship.

The Hotels

The 1895 Championship was notable for a reason other than golf. In 1894 *The Bulger* had carried an article which stated – 'In the Stotfield district many buildings, we believe, are in the architects' hands, and will be erected in due course. On Monday the first turf was cut for the foundation of a new hotel, which will without question be a great convenience to the West End. The prospect of the extension of the town is one to make the citizens glad and hopeful of greater activity and life in the community. Let Lossiemouth grow and flourish!' William Christie, the enterprising Elgin hotelier, was the sixth club Captain in 1894-5 and he had taken careful note of the enthusiastic crowds of spectators and the large numbers of very good golfers entered for the first Championship. In 1895, with great foresight he built, opposite the Moray clubhouse, the magnificent Stotfield Hotel which, with its 70 bedrooms was full year after year until the 1950s. The great majority of guests booked their accommodation for the following year before they left. The Stotfield was so successful that in 1903 a second large hotel was built near at hand and named the Marine Hotel and it quickly enjoyed a similar success.

MARINE AND STOTFIELD HOTELS, LOSSIEMOUTH.

Sir Alexander Grant

A shareholder in the Marine Hotel, Sir Alexander Grant of the Scottish biscuit firm McVitie & Price, kept a fine suite of rooms there for most of the year and when he was in residence he frequently had his own professional, Ted Ray, as his guest. Ted Ray and Harry Vardon were the only golfers to win both the Open Championship and the U.S. Open Championship until Tony Jacklin in 1970. Edward (Ted) Ray was a huge lumbering figure of a man who hurled himself into the ball with all his power. His philosophy of golf was encapsulated in answer to a question frequently asked of him about how to hit the ball further when he would reply; 'hit it a bloody sight harder, mate' – but it is doubtful if he ever said that to his employer. In 1920 Ray won the United States Open at Inverness, Toledo, and O.B. Keeler described the final hole:

> He pitched on to the green well away from the cup and his approach was short, leaving him more than a yard from the hole. It was here that he got the news that this putt carried the championship as far as Vardon was concerned. He was preparing to putt when he got it. He promptly handed his club back to his caddy; removed the habitual pipe from his mouth; and while the assembled thousands fairly sweated blood with anxiety, he calmly refilled his pipe, lighted it, puffed away two or three times, took back his putter from the caddy, and without any more to-do, sent down the putt that made him champion.*

Alexander Grant, a great friend of Ramsay MacDonald, was a staunch supporter of the Moray club and put up large sums of money for the McVitie & Price professional tournaments held there in 1920 and 1922 and which attracted large fields with prize money in excess of £800, and a first prize almost twice that offered in the Open. The winner of the McVitie & Price cup in 1922 was Joe Kirkwood of Australia who won by 13 strokes and took the first prize of £130 - £55 more than the first prize for the Open.

Some Changes

In 1897, in Queen Victoria's Jubilee Year, the fourth year of the Championship, the format was changed with 36 holes medal play and eight qualifiers deciding the winner by match play. The following year there were 16 qualifiers, but it was not until 1986 that the Council decided on 32 qualifiers for all three sections – low and high handicap sections had been competed for since 1949 and 1968 – and that remains the settled and successful system to the present day.

The rubber-cored Haskell ball had appeared in 1902 and although the professionals initially did not like it, golfers of more moderate skills

---

The Bobby Jones Story by Keeler & Rice (The Fireside Press, London 1955)

were enthusiastic and it was not long before it was universally adopted. The introduction of the Haskell ball resulted in a great deal of controversy and initially it was banned by Dornoch and some Glasgow golf clubs. The majority of seaside links had been laid out for the gutty ball and recognising this, the noted amateur golfer John L. Low of St Andrews and Nairn announced that 'now the holes at St Andrews are within the compass of infirm old men'.

Robert Harris 1904

A Notable Scalp

J. Gordon Simpson of the R&A won the Northern in 1903. In the final he defeated J.A. Donaldson of Aberdeen Bon-Accord who was fresh from his triumph over Harold Hilton in the Cruden Bay Amateur Tournament. This was a notable scalp for an Aberdeen golfer as Hilton had been twice Open champion before winning the British Amateur in 1900 and 1901. Donaldson competed frequently at Lossiemouth but failed to win the title. Gordon Simpson gained nine Scottish international caps before playing in the inaugural match against the USA at Hoylake in 1921 which was the forerunner of the Walker Cup. George Duncan, the famous Aberdeen-born golfer who became personal professional to the old Aga Khan, caddied as a boy at the Links course in Aberdeen for Jimmy Donaldson, 'our crack amateur, who later turned professional and went to America'. Duncan later met up with Donaldson who was one of the prominent golfers in the field in the 1922 American Open and in the Western New York Open which Duncan won by five strokes from Walter Hagen*.

Robert Harris

Probably the most successful golfer to win the Northern Amateur was the young Robert Harris of Carnoustie in 1904. Already a much travelled and experienced golfer he went on to appear in three British Amateur Championship finals, being beaten by Harold Hilton at St Andrews and Roger Wethered at Deal, but finally winning at Westward Ho! in 1925. In the following year of 1926 he was beaten by Bobby Jones, the greatest American amateur of all time. Although he had to travel by sea on the *Aquitania* Jones, in 1926, became the first man to win both the British and American Open championships and in a period of only 17 days. In 1930 Bobby Jones won both the British and American Open and Amateur Championships – the 'Impregnable Quadrilateral' according to O. B. Keeler, or the first Grand Slam – and retired trailing clouds of glory at the tender age of 28 years.

The 18ᵗʰ Hole

In the 1905 Northern Championship, Clive Lawrence of Woking, son of Mr Justice Lawrence, Recorder of Windsor, and a past captain of the Cambridge University side, met and defeated C.A. Macpherson whose father was also a judge in Edinburgh. Macpherson was the brother of Dr Lewis W. Macpherson who had won the inaugural Northern Amateur in 1894 and subsequently retained possession of the original Championship trophy by winning it three times. Lawrence had learned to play his golf at Woking but he played out of Nairn where he lived in the summer months. In a practice round for this meeting, the Hon. Archie Gordon, an Oxford blue and son of Lord Aberdeen, was playing

Golf At The Gallop by George Duncan (London 1951)

17

with Raymond Asquith and Sir James Simpson when he holed his second shot with an iron at the 400 yard 18th hole. This was the first time the hole had been achieved in two shots and he received a warm welcome from the spectators above the green.

In his *Good Golf Guide to Scotland* (1982) David Hamilton selects his 18 best links holes.

Lossiemouth 18th (423 yds)

Surely [this is] the noblest finishing hole in Scotland. The drive is along a valley overlooked by the gracious Stotfield houses with the Moray Firth and dunes to the left. The second shot must gain some height to reach the plateau green set in a natural amphitheatre in front of the solid clubhouse. The green is also beside the main street, and hence a small, well-informed audience is usually present to watch attempts at this difficult second shot.*

The population of Lossiemouth turn out for the presentation in 1905

Two more Scottish internationals were winners of the Northern Amateur: [Dr] F.H. Scroggie of Carnoustie in 1906 and Gordon Lockhart of Prestwick St Nicholas in 1907. Lockhart was again the winner in 1908 beating the Cambridge captain V.C. Longstaffe (Aldeburgh) on his way to the final. A semi-finalist in the British Amateur of 1911, he won his

*Now *The Scottish Golf Guide* – Canongate Books Ltd (1995)

first cap for Scotland in the same year and also the much sought after Edward Trophy at Glasgow Gailes before winning the Irish Open Amateur in 1912. After turning professional in 1921 Lockhart was appointed by Gleneagles Hotel as their first professional.

The secretary's report on the 1908 Championship demonstrated the widespread popularity of Lossiemouth's far-sighted approach in

Frank Scroggie 1906

instigating a major Championship in Scotland. He noted that the entrants included members of Royal Dornoch, Royal Aberdeen, Inverness, Nairn, Mid-Surrey, Royal Wimbledon, Deal, Tantallon, Mount Charles in County Donegal, Muswell Hill, Princes, Mortonhall and many other golf clubs. The Moray Golf Club's Northern Amateur Championship at Lossiemouth had become a well-established part of Britain's golfing calendar.

Donald Grant of Royal Dornoch

John Sutherland, scratch golfer and the famous secretary of Royal Dornoch for over 50 years, played a prominent part as a competitor from the beginning. Another scratch golfer, and noted publicist for Dornoch, Donald Grant was the victor in 1909 beating Lieut W.D. Allan of Moray, who was the first Lossiemouth club member to have reached the final. In his short book, *Personal Memories of Royal Dornoch Golf Club 1900-1925*, which has a foreword by Tom Watson, Donald Grant relates his story of the Northern Championship in 1909.

> Returned from Hamburg across the North Sea to Firth of Forth, I cabled my entry to Lossiemouth for the Northern Championship. There were far fewer tournaments then. I stayed with an uncle at Findrassie Farm, Elgin, borrowed a bicycle for my five miles into Lossiemouth each day, and picked up my own seven clubs at the pro's shop there. From my Northern Counties Cup play at Lossie in 1906 I had some knowledge of the golf course and I liked it. I felt I was playing for Dornoch as much as for myself. I duly qualified after two rounds medal play.

> Two more days of really keen match play followed: but first of all there was the sweepstake at five bob a head. "Old John Birnie", golfer and Provost of Inverness, drew my name in the sweepstake, more than happy to have a Dornoch golfer, he knew me personally, of course. I played good confident golf; to this day I remember some of my chip shots. My second and third round matches were the toughest. D G Mackenzie (+2) Mortonhall, Edinburgh I met in the second round and got through, then I had to play a more notable golfer (and well I knew it), Gordon Lockhart, Troon, a Scots international golfer who later became pro at Gleneagles. I managed to beat him too, but it was a close match and I still remember it. The final was not so hard a match. I noticed however, that I was pale and sort of haggard at the end of the three days of mounting concentration, as match followed keen match.

Donald Grant was a prominent member of the Dornoch four-man team which won the Northern Counties Cup in eleven successive years 1902-1913, a record which still stands to this day.

A New Course Record

George Thomson broke the course record with a 70 in 1910 but this was lowered three weeks later when the Scottish Professional Championship came to Lossiemouth and was won by Tom Fernie of Troon with a score of 291 – fifteen strokes ahead of his nearest rival. In his second round of 65 he set a mark which remained the course record for almost 90 years until it was lowered to the current level of 64 by Lorne Kelly of Cowal in the Scottish Open Amateur Stroke Play Championship of 1998. It seems unlikely that any other seaside links course can have had such a long-standing record. Fernie's score is worth setting out, and one must remember that it was done with the poor quality early Haskell ball and hand-made hickory shafted clubs, far removed from the precisely engineered clubs and golf balls of today. Without a watering system the greens were as keen as ice and putting often presented a real problem. The course in 1910 was 6000 yards long and the bogey (par) was 79.

THE MORAY GOLF CLUB.

Competition *Scottish Professional Championship (Brahms)*

Mr *J. RO. Fernie*

Bogey.	Names of Holes.	Yds.	Strokes.	
3	1. Mt. Lebanon - - -	216	3	
5	2. Cup - - - - - -	426	5	
5	3. Table - - - - -	421	3	
4	4. Coulart - - - -	206	4	
5	5. Kinneddar - - -	420	4	
3	6. Gordonstoun - - -	130	3	
5	7. Ring - - - - -	459	4	
5	8. Heather - - - -	433	4	
4	9. Ditch - - - - -	290	3	33
4	10. St. Gerardine - -	266	3	
4	11. Lighthouse - - -	271	3	
4	12. Beacon - - - -	305	4	
5	13. V - - - - - -	466	4	
5	14. Sea - - - - - -	263	4	
3	15. Short - - - - -	166	2	
5	16. Road - - - - -	372	4	
5	17. Long - - - - -	490	4	
5	18. Home - - - - -	400	4	
79		6000		32

TOTAL 65

HANDICAP ....

HANDICAP SCORE........... 65

A Great Year

1911 was one of the great years for the Championship. Well over 100 golfers were entered and of these, 30 were playing off scratch or better. The qualifying rounds were played in such a boisterous North-West wind that the bogey of 80 for a difficult seaside links was rarely threatened. As usual the entry featured players from all parts of the country with another Dornoch invasion of eight scratch golfers led by Donald Grant. The wealth of Dornoch talent at this time was epitomised by the gentleman amateur Charles E. (Charlie) Dick, a Scottish international, whose home course was Royal Liverpool but who was an occasional visitor to Dornoch. He reached the last eight of the British Amateur five times, and in 1907 he won the St George's Challenge Cup at the Royal St George's club at Sandwich, joining a select band including Robert Harris in 1905, the year after he had won the Championship at Lossiemouth. Jack Nicklaus as an amateur won the same trophy in 1959.

[Sir] E.W. Holderness, an Oxford blue and future British Amateur Champion scored 90 in his first round at Lossiemouth but failed to return a card in his second round. Colin C. Aylmer of Devon, beaten finalist in the British Amateur of 1910 and playing out of Strathpeffer, handled the conditions best of all and returned 79 and 80 for a total of 159. However, George Thomson of Moray, playing his best golf, took Aylmer's scalp on his way to the final against C.E. Dick, but eventually had to give best to a battle-hardened competitor.

Caddies at the 1st tee circa 1913

The Caddies

Obtaining a caddie to carry the clubs was never a problem at Lossiemouth as a large number of boys, and some older caddies, were always available. They looked for visitors and the well-to-do 'shotters' who took a break from the grouse moors some time after the 12th of August for a day's golfing and were known to be free with their money. A serious blow was dealt the older lads in September 1912 when the Council took the decision not to employ caddies over 16 years of age because of the liability of the golf club to pay insurance. Herbert Asquith – Prime Minister of the Liberal government and a prominent member at Moray – with his Chancellor David Lloyd George, proposed the 1911 National Insurance Act. This gave the British working classes the first contributory system of insurance against illness and unemployment. All wage-earners between 16 and 70 had to join the health scheme in which each worker paid fourpence a week and the employer added threepence and the state twopence. The caddies were on their own, but their fees were carefully watched.

At the Annual General Meeting of the club the following March, Dr John Taylor of Elgin complained that 'the caddies were overpaid and inefficient' since the 25% increase in their remuneration to bring them into line with other clubs. The Captain, Mr J.H. Hair, defended the caddies, who, the Council felt, were considerably underpaid compared to those at Nairn, Inverness, Dornoch and Aberdeen. Hence the 25% increase from 10 pence to one shilling and a penny per round.

The most famous of the Lossiemouth caddies was Jimmie ('Dame') Main who lived to be over 90 years of age. Main caddied for many fine golfers at Lossiemouth and particularly those famous golfers who spent some time in the summer months as guests of the Tennant family at Innes House near Elgin. The Innes Tennants are closely related to the Tennant family of North Berwick, who were well known industrialists, and whose doyen, Sir Charles Tennant, Bt., was a past Captain of The Glasgow Golf Club at Killermont and donor of the Tennant Cup, the oldest amateur golfing trophy in the world. Colonel Edward Tennant was Captain of the Moray Golf Club for three years from 1935 and Roger Wethered and his sister Joyce were frequent visitors. Main recalls caddying for Joyce, when at the third hole, – with the old tee on the other side of the road – she put her second shot in the bunker on the right side of the green, two long shots for a man let alone a woman. Ever since, this bunker has been known as 'Joyce Wethered's bunker'.

He also caddied for another visitor to Innes, namely Major C.K. (Cis) Hutchison of Sandwich, a Scottish international for nine years in succession and runner-up in the British Amateur of 1909, who played in the Northern Championship in some wild weather and failed to qualify.

Sir Iain Tennant made the principal speech at the Centenary dinner of the Moray Golf Club in 1989 and in his address he said:

My father, a mad keen golfer, was a great friend of Joyce Wethered, as she then was. Joyce used to come and stay at Lochnabo, and later, at Innes, together with C.K.(Cis) Hutchison, another famous golfer of the time. They played golf all day and talked golf all night. Before leaving for the course each morning, they practised their swings on the lawn and took movies of each other, which were studied at the next visit. I still have some of these movies. ...Joyce, who is now 87, married the late Sir John Heathcote Amory and lives in Devon. I told her of tonight's celebration and she has sent the following message.

"I am so interested to hear that the Lossiemouth Golf Club is about to celebrate its 100th anniversary. I would like to send my sincere congratulations, if I may, and best wishes for another 100 years. I still remember those enjoyable days – if alas, not very often – I can still picture the last exciting shot up to the 18th green – a grand finish to the course. Golf on seaside links will always be the best and are very special in Scotland. I have to live on memories these days – among many very happy ones were my visits to Innes House and golf at Lossiemouth. Do pass on my congratulations to the members on their hundredth birthday." *

George Thomson

George Thomson was far and away the best amateur golfer produced by the Moray Golf Club in its first forty years. Born in 1890, he was to follow in his father's footsteps as a chemist in Elgin and always had to work for a living, unlike many of the amateurs he encountered in his playing career. He broke the Moray course record at the age of 15 and won the club championship at 16. He was club champion for six consecutive years and 11 times in all up to 1926, a record which endured for almost 60 years. At the age of 16 and playing off scratch he entered his first Northern Amateur and reached the semi-final. Often favourite to win on his own course, the Championship eluded him until, in 1913, he became the first member of the Moray club in 20 years to take the title. Thomson had previously won the

*Sir Iain Tennant, K.T., of Innes House. Personal communication.

Cruden Bay and Nairn tournaments in 1908 and in reaching the Nairn final again in 1910 he had beaten Major C.K. Hutchison, the runner-up in the British Amateur of 1909. After the Great War Thomson appeared in the final again in 1921 but was beaten by G.C. Manford of Luffness New. Playing from Edinburgh University, Manford in 1914 won the last Northern Championship before the Great War.

Thomson's father had prepared his famous emulsion of cod liver oil and sold it as *Thomson's Cod Liver Oil Cream*, which, according to letters received from their representatives, was highly regarded by the Tsar of Russia, the 90 year-old Florence Nightingale, Queen Elizabeth when Duchess of York, and the young Princesses Elizabeth and Margaret Rose. All were said to have benefited greatly from the cream which, in the days of empirical medicine, was taken in large amounts by patients suffering from colds, influenza, coughs and chest complaints. Doubtless the small amount of spirits in the recipe had an extra fortifying effect.

The Tsar's brother, His Imperial Highness Grand Duke Michael of Russia, not only founded the golf club at Cannes but was also an enthusiastic golfer at St Andrews and a prominent member of the R&A. It may be that he heard of the well-known cream when he was playing golf in Scotland and took back a bottle or two for his brother – but this is simply speculation.

> *"The game is ancient, manly and employs*
> *In its departments, women, men and boys,*
> *Men play the game, the boys the clubs convey,*
> *And lovely women give the prize away."* *

---

*George Fullerton Carnegie's poem 'Golfiana' c. 1833.

George Thomson – the first Moray winner of the Northern Amateur Championship receives the trophy from Miss Asquith, 1913
A policeman in attendance to guard against suffragettes

CHAPTER THREE
After the Great War of 1914-19

The enormous loss of life among the combatants was followed by the disastrous influenza pandemic of 1918 which killed more people than the Great War itself. At somewhere between 20 and 40 million people dead it has been cited as the most devastating epidemic in recorded world history. More people died of influenza in a single year than in four years of the Bubonic Plague [Black Death] from 1347 to 1351. Known as 'Spanish Flu' or 'La Grippe' the influenza of 1918-19 was a global disaster. Everybody was glad to get back to some sort of normality and this applied to sport in particular.

The Northern Championship was not held until 1920 when the first all-Moray final took place and Captain Kynoch Cumming defeated A.G. Campbell in the final. Cumming took the scalp of Dr William Tweddell of Aberdeen University in the quarter finals. Tweddell had been twice wounded in the war and had won the Military Cross and Bar. Although he was a stern competitor he failed to win in repeated attempts at Lossiemouth. He did however win the British Amateur Championship of 1927 at Hoylake and in 1935 he was again in the final at Royal Lytham where he met the holder Lawson Little of America. Bernard Darwin saw this match which was refereed by Robert Harris.*

> Now for 1934 and 1935 and two American victories running won by the same player who was in the same two years Amateur Champion of his own country. I feel that the brush should be dipped in earthquake and eclipse to do justice to Lawson Little, for here was a player for whom my hard-worked epithet 'formidable' is scarcely strong enough: Lawson was intimidating. Not very tall but enormously broad and enormously strong, capable of a daunting pugnacity of expression, he was as a bull in the long game, and yet no dove could be gentler near the hole, so persuasive was his touch. The power of his rather shut-faced swing was immense, at the top of the swing, with everything at full stretch, he looked as if he must surely kill the ball, and he was essentially a killer in match play.

Between Two Wars by Bernard Darwin (Chatto & Windus 1944)

...this final at St Anne's was a wonderful match which saw him fighting with his back to the wall against a truly heroic Tweddell, to emerge victorious at the last hole.

In 1921 and 1922 G.C. Manford won his second and third Northern Amateur Championships and was capped for Scotland. In the 1922 final he defeated Welsh international Seymour Noon. In 1923 W.C. White was the winner, and also the eighth Mortonhall player to appear in the final.

Unfortunately, in 1923 the Scottish Golf Union requested that the use of the word 'Championship' should be restricted to the national open and amateur championships of Scotland, and Lossiemouth acquiesced and changed the title of the Northern Amateur Championship to the Moray Open. Thus one of the most successful Amateur Championships in the British Isles since 1894 became the Moray Open Amateur Tournament.

The Railway

The change of title in no way diminished the enthusiasm of those golfers and their families and friends who had been coming to holiday and compete at Lossiemouth, the Brighton of the North, for so many years. Indeed, such was the enthusiasm of the golfers that the railway authorities decided that the demand could only be met by the introduction of a direct weekly sleeping car between London King's Cross and Lossiemouth via Aberdeen to ease the passage to Lossiemouth of both golfers and visitors during the summer. Leaving London at 8.00 p.m., the sleeping car was attached to an express which went straight through to Aberdeen. From there it left at exactly 7.45 a.m., with the recently introduced breakfast-car attached, and Elgin was reached via Craigellachie at 9.56 a.m., and finally Lossiemouth at 10.20 a.m. At more than 600 miles this was at that time the longest through service in Britain. Ian Peebles, the Test cricketer – whose father was minister at Birnie Kirk in Moray – in his book *Spinners Yarn*, recalls getting on this dining–car in Aberdeen and breakfasting on fresh herrings done in oatmeal and accompanied by warm, fluffy baps. Peebles was born in Aberdeen and played for the M.C.C. and England and in 1931 Wisden voted him Test cricketer of the year.*

The Ramsay MacDonald Affair

In 1924 A.G. Campbell, the Burghead schoolmaster, became only the third Moray player in 30 years to win in front of his home crowd by defeating Willis Mackenzie of Mortonhall, the reigning Scottish Amateur Champion, in the final. Mackenzie had won his title earlier in the summer in the first national championship ever played at the Royal Aberdeen golf club.

This was accomplished against the background of the widespread

Spinners Yarn. I. A. R. Peebles (London 1977)

28

local and national publicity (not to say scandal) attendant on the Moray club's failure to reinstate Ramsay MacDonald who had become the first ever Labour Prime Minister in that year. The Moray club had expelled MacDonald for his pacifist (and perhaps political) views in 1916. A well-publicised meeting at the Burgh Court House in Elgin to reinstate him in 1924 had failed, as the club was unable to persuade the necessary two-thirds majority of members of the need for MacDonald's reinstatement. And so the Prime Minister of Great Britain remained *persona non grata* at the Moray Golf Club in his native Lossiemouth, the town of his birth. He had transferred his allegiance to the golf course at Spey Bay near Fochabers and when he became Premier again in 1929 he resisted further attempts to entice him back.

Ramsay MacDonald at the starter's box with Alister and Malcolm, 1909

MacDonald's final correspondence on the matter was with his friend Captain James Brander Dunbar, Laird of Pitgaveny and the superior of Lossiemouth: affectionately known by the locals as 'The Lairdie'.

Pitgaveny, Elgin, Scotland
June 28th 1929

My dear Premier,

....I was home wounded in 1916 and raised my voice loud against the then action of the Club. I have thus taken a consistent line throughout which makes walking easy. I take it that you must be privy to what is going on, for knowing the character of my J.R. MacD. as I do, I feel certain that he is just the man to tell them to "go to hell". I would also.

Anyhow, don't bother to answer this UNLESS you wish me to act for you: If I don't hear I'll leave the idiots who made the mess to damned well lick it up.

Yours aye,
J.B. Dunbar

Monday 1 July

Captain J.B. Dunbar
Pitgaveny, Elgin

My dear Laird,

Thank you so much for your letter and its enclosure. [Notice of the meeting]. I want the members to be left absolutely alone and to consider nothing but what they feel it is their duty to do regarding the existence of the banning resolution. As a matter of fact I do not come into it at all. They have had any number of opportunities to put things right within the last few years, and once they definitely declined to do so. Now, everybody laughs at them and the existence of the resolution humiliates them, not me. What they are therefore proposing to do is get themselves out of a fix...

I enjoy the Spey Bay course and so do my friends. It came to my rescue in 1916 and I am not a man to treat any friends of mine as a mere convenience. Therefore I stick to Spey Bay.

Yours sincerely,
J. Ramsay MacDonald*

Two Champions

Willis Mackenzie, who played twice in the Walker Cup, won the Scottish Amateur again in 1928 and Jack Bookless succeeded him in 1929. Bookless (Inverness and Moray) was a competitor on more than one occasion at Lossiemouth and he won the Moray title in 1925 when he beat J.G. Rowan (Drumpellier) in the final. John Birnie Jnr. of Inverness was the winner in 1927 and recalled how his father, the Provost of Inverness, had drawn Donald Grant of Dornoch in the then 'five bob' sweepstake when Grant won in 1909. Local men began to figure

The Moray Golf Club at Lossiemouth by John McConachie (Moravian Press, Elgin 1988)

more frequently in the tournament around this time. J.L. Laing was runner-up to John Birnie, Hugo Ronald won in 1930, and schoolmaster Alec McKenzie was defeated in the 1931 final by H. McMaster of Old Ranfurly – a club which was home to many fine Scottish golfers.

Jack Bookless, winner in 1925

John Birnie Jnr and Bobby Jones, at the British Amateur Championship, Muirfield 1926

More Equipment Changes

Following the introduction of the rubber-cored golf ball, another important change in equipment occurred in 1929 with the introduction of steel shafts to replace the old wooden hickory-shafted golf clubs which had been in use by club-makers for eighty years. Steel shafts were standardised and much more robust and were already fitted to the heads, whereas hickory shafts were often fitted to the player at his club and frequently required maintenance and repairs. In America steel shafts had been legal since 1926 and most professionals used them, although the great amateur Bobby Jones used a complete set of hickory-shafted clubs in his Grand Slam year of 1930. In 1932 the United States Golf Association set standards for the golf ball which were later adopted on this side of the Atlantic resulting in a ball weighing a maximum of 1.620 oz. and with a diameter of not less than 1.680 inches.

As we have seen, local golfers began to feature more prominently in the tournament around this time, and a very fine golfer in the 42 year-old Lossiemouth secondary school headmaster Dr J.C. Jessop recorded a hat trick of victories in 1934-36-39. His fourth and final victory was achieved in 1949 at the age of 57. Jessop not only played in both the British Amateur and Open Championships, but for the *Teach Yourself* series he wrote a popular instruction book called *Teach Yourself Golf* which ran to six editions and can still be purchased. However, some of his pithier stories have been edited out. In the original text Jessop related the story of Sandy Herd playing at Carnoustie with Andra Kirkaldy as his caddie. As Herd was approaching his ball about to play

Dr J. C. Jessop, 1958

his second shot, Kirkaldy handed him his brassie. 'Give me my cleek, Andra,' said Sandy, 'I haven't got a very good stance.' 'Play your brassie' brusquely retorted Kirkaldy, 'You play this game wi' yer heid, no' yer feet.'

Dick Walker

The winner of the Moray Open in 1933-35-37 was an extraordinary character. R.S. (Dick) Walker was educated at Winchester School and Oxford University where he was a triple blue. Although he did not play golf at Oxford, when he came to Aberdeen University to study divinity he attacked the game with remarkable enthusiasm. In those days the study of divinity left plenty of time for golf and Walker took full advantage of it. In the summer-time he lived in a caravan by the 18th hole at Cruden Bay Golf course near Aberdeen and practised assiduously – it is said that he hit 1000 balls every day. His short grooved swing was simple and very effective and in 1933 and 1935 he won at Lossiemouth by beating the Scottish international Donald Cameron of Kirkintilloch on each occasion. Dick Walker entered the 1933 British Amateur Championship at Hoylake and reached the last eight before being eliminated. In his usual unconventional way he pitched a tent on the beach and lived there for a week. The winner was the 54 year old Michael Scott whose brother Osmund had been runner-up in 1905 and whose sister Lady Margaret Scott had won the Ladies' Amateur Championship in 1893-4-5 and then retired without any more fields left to conquer.

In 1934 Walker won the Scottish Universities' Championship, followed by a string of local events including the Scottish Northern Open Championships of 1934-35 in which he took on and defeated the professionals. He always wore a fisherman's jersey and never felt the need to employ a caddy, preferring to carry his own clubs which were far fewer than the 14 allowed today. In 1935 he won the first of his five international caps. At Lossiemouth in 1937 he defeated a tough competitor in dentist Harvey Mackintosh of Royal Aberdeen. According to Colin Farquharson, Walker more or less gave up golf for many years – not, as has been suggested, due to his failure to be chosen for the Walker Cup team, but because he married his sweetheart Elizabeth the following year and found that there was more to life than golf. He and his wife went to Johannesburg after the war to teach the Alexander technique of physical education, and after some 13 years without golf Dick Walker took up the game again and added to his golfing laurels in South Africa.*

At one time, at Aberdeen University, the study of divinity was occasionally seen as a way into the study of medicine, as it was comparatively easy in those days to change courses. If the student was a particularly good golfer that would stand him in good stead with

*Aberdeen Press & Journal, March 1989

33

the medical faculty, as most of the professors were themselves keen students of the game. In the history of Royal Aberdeen Golf Club, Lewis Middleton had this to say of a fellow past captain:

> J.W.L. Bain became captain in 1960. He was a great character. It was reputed that he was the beneficiary of a trust set up by his father whereby he had an income of £300 per year provided he matriculated at the University. This was a fair sum of money in the early thirties so John studied divinity for years, which was not only the cheapest subject but also gave him plenty of time for his main interests, golf, rugby and cattle dealing. John eventually took up medicine and sailed through all his exams.*

The five year domination of the tournament by Walker and Jessop ended in the penultimate tournament before the War when K.B. Murray of Eastwood beat the 25 year-old John S. Montgomerie (Cambuslang) in the final. After the war Montgomerie won the Scottish Amateur in 1957 and was capped for Scotland. A Walker cup selector and noted administrator, he was president of the Scottish Golf Union in 1965. As we have seen Dr Jessop defeated Alec Coburn, the Aberdeen University captain, in the last tournament before the outbreak of much more serious hostilities.

The Walker Cup

The Walker Cup, and its predecessor in 1921, before and after the two world wars, has featured a number of prominent golfers who have appeared in the Northern Championship, and its successor the Moray Open, including Robert Harris who captained the British Walker Cup team in three successive matches. Others include J. Gordon Simpson, Sir Ernest Holderness, Colin C. Aylmer, W. Willis Mackenzie, Dr William Tweddell and Hugh Stuart – with a number of these players representing their country on more than one occasion.

Royal Aberdeen Golf Club – 200 Years of Golf by J.A.G. Mearns 1980

CHAPTER FOUR
Beyond the Second World War of 1939-45

The aerodrome built on the outskirts of Lossiemouth immediately before the War was soon in use by the Royal Air Force to train aircrews for Bomber Command, and among a number of important missions undertaken from there was the sinking of the German battleship *Tirpitz* in a Norwegian fiord by a squadron of Lancaster bombers. The fog-free climate and the generally fine weather in the area of the Moray Firth was found to be ideal for aircrew and pilot training and this did not present a problem for golfers until the invention of the jet engine by Air Commodore Sir Frank Whittle. The Royal Navy's Fleet Air Arm became the tenants as *H.M.S. Fulmar* in 1946 and the Royal Air Force returned in 1972. This undoubtedly led to the decline of Lossiemouth as a holiday resort, and golfers and their families recall how the Stotfield Hotel remained popular with the same visitors for a number of years after the war, but the aircraft noise soon forced a change of attitude. Although the 18 holes of the Old Course remained in the top ten British courses for a number of years the experts who made the selections dropped it from their lists after a number of unfortunate experiences with low flying aircraft.

The Golf Ball Incident

One small incident lightened the occasional gloom induced by the over-flying aircraft and is now recorded in the *Golfers' Handbook*. In June 1971, playing in an Elgin Academy staff versus pupils match and partnered by Farquhar Thomson, Martin Robertson didn't get an eagle on the ninth hole, but he almost got a jet aircraft. From the ninth tee the 27 year-old schoolteacher hit a high drive and the ball smacked into the fuselage of a Navy Hunter jet coming into land at the base. The base issued the following terse communiqué:- 'All our aircraft returned safely' said a spokesman, 'but it is understood that one of their golf balls is missing'.

Post-War Rationing

Few people will now remember the immediate post-war conditions for the general population. Britain had not only lost an Empire but had dissipated its financial reserves in helping to win the war. New motorcars were not to be had and there was rationing of petrol, food, bread and spirits along with a shortage of suitable holiday accommodation. The Attlee government had introduced bread rationing as late as July of 1947 with two bread units equalling one small loaf of 14 oz.. Golf balls were scarce and competitors in serious competitions were given certificates to enable them to buy the rationed golf balls at local shops. Eric Brown, a great favourite at Lossiemouth and winner of the Scottish Amateur at Carnoustie in 1946, said that before the event he 'tramped the whole of Montrose and into every sports shop' looking for balls but all he managed to accumulate was one new ball. During the championship itself every qualifier was given a chit which enabled him to buy two new balls.[*]

Lossie's Bill Campbell played in this Scottish Amateur and recalls a connection to Brown's victory.

> I had bought a ticket in the selling sweep, just like the one we have in Lossie. I could not get down to the clubhouse for the auction so I delegated a friend to act for me. He came back and said he could not get in so he didn't know whether I had drawn a ticket or not. When I got home I found a cheque for, I think, sixty pounds – the first prize on the unexpected winner, an unknown railway fireman, Eric Brown. I used the money to buy a set of Nicoll's 'Pinsplitters', the first match set I ever owned.

Members of the golf club were overjoyed when the Council announced that on Christmas Day 1947 and New Year's Day 1948 all members (apart from juniors) could have four small nips of whisky, and that the rationing of gin would be abandoned on these days. Because of the demand and the shortage of whisky and gin the club had difficulty in honouring this rather rash promise.

Return to Competition

But the War's end ushered in a social revolution at the golf club and the men who had thrown out Ramsay MacDonald were no longer so influential in the affairs of the club. This became evident in a few short years with the Council and its office-bearers beginning to reflect the composition of the local population. Fishermen, who for so long had had found it difficult to become members because of the nature of their occupation, joined in large numbers. So it was entirely fitting

Knave Of Clubs by Eric Brown (London 1961)

that the first Moray Open after the war in 1947 should be won by a local fisherman George T. Murray who defeated A.J.D. (Bunny) Blaikie of Royal Musselburgh in the final. Blaikie was no mean golfer having already won the much sought after Craw's Nest Tassie, which was played for annually at Carnoustie.

As had happened after the first Great War there was a strong desire to return to normal in sporting events, and golf was no exception. Young men who had been keen golfers prior to the war were anxious to get to grips with the game again, to hone their skills and play some competitive golf.

A Stymie

One such was ex-naval officer and local man W.D. (Bill) Campbell. A friendly and gregarious man he was always an enthusiastic competitor who threw himself into the summer golfing encounters which took place in open tournaments around the Moray coast. He won the Moray Open in 1948 and again in 1951 when he defeated in the final a tall, determined golfer who was out to emulate his renowned father George Thomson, the first Moray member to win the Northern in 1913. Dr Horace Thomson was a powerful hitter of a golf ball but he ran into Campbell at his best and lost to him at the 17th hole in the final. Bill Campbell emigrated to Toronto where he took an accounting degree and was Treasurer of a large printing company before he switched to teaching accounting at Humber College for the last seven years of his working life. Returning to Lossiemouth 40 years later to play (and qualify) in another Moray Open and meeting his 1951 opponent, there was much jocular talk about the stymie [a long forgotten penalty] he had laid on the second green which cost Thomson the hole – and, according to Thomson, possibly the match.

Over the hundred years of the match play stages it seems clear that good match players have a hidden vein of hostility in their make up. Not, it must be said, a personal hostility to the golfers they meet; rather a desire to measure themselves against a foeman they recognise as worthy of their steel. Match play has long been a part of amateur championships which demands certain qualities of character in a player, such as the ability to withstand the pressure of an opponent's unexpected long putt or chip shot holed. Conflict between man and man is the fundamental nature of match play which makes it such compelling viewing.

Ladies Enter the Open Tournament

The Moray Open had been largely a male preserve but in 1949 the ladies sprung a surprise when Chrystal McGeagh of the home club won the low handicap section. Irish Ladies' Champion in 1939 and an Irish international both before and after the second war, Miss McGeagh relished taking on the men and it was probably no great surprise that she was successful. She followed this up in 1950 by winning the Silver Jubilee Challenge Cup (open to ladies and gentlemen) which was awarded to the player with the best medal score under handicap.

In the twentieth century, from 1904 up to 1951, the Moray Golf Club had no fewer than eight women members who between them collected 22 international caps for Scotland, England and Ireland. One was Meg Farquhar who had been an assistant in 1929 to the great Lossiemouth teaching professional George Smith who coached many of the international players. In 1933 she became the first woman professional to play in a national open Championship in Britain when she acquitted herself well when playing at her native Lossiemouth in the Scottish Professional Championship. The newspapers reported that she had played with a set of hickory-shafted irons and as a result of the attendant publicity she was invited to the firm of Accles & Pollock Ltd and presented with a set of steel-shafted clubs made by Nicoll of Leven. Meg Farquhar Main had been reinstated as an amateur in 1950 and that year almost managed to emulate Chrystal McGeagh but was beaten in the final of the low handicap section.

James Lindsay

A long-standing visitor to Lossiemouth, James Lindsay of Falkirk Tryst, was runner-up in 1952 and winner of the trophy in 1953. Lindsay had an outstanding record as a top flight golfer having won the British Boys' Amateur Championship two years in succession in 1929 and 1930: a feat unsurpassed to this day except by one other golfer, the little known R.W. Peattie of Cupar in Fife. Lindsay was selected for Scotland in all the Home Internationals from 1933 through to 1936 and in 1934 at Glasgow Golf Club he won the Tennant Cup (established in 1880) which is the oldest amateur competition in the world. In the 1953 final at Lossiemouth he defeated a fine Moray and Elgin golfer in Ian Rodger who went on to take the title in 1963. Lindsay used his experience and talents to good effect as a golf administrator and eventually became President of the Scottish Golf Union.

Young Blood

The palm had now passed to a new generation of home-bred young lions who had first learned and sharpened their games on the links at Lossie. These young men hit the ball hard; and more importantly for a links course they hit it long and straight. They were of course Christopher J. Macleod and the Thomson brothers: Farquhar and his younger brother Alistair. First up was CJ – very long and very straight with a swing which could not be faulted. In 1954 as an 18 year-old schoolboy he defeated the 19 year-old Farquhar Thomson in the semi-

Chris Macleod

final of the Moray Open. In the final he met a tidy player, D.F. Beatson of Edinburgh, and far out-drove him, but his putting was ruinous with four three putts in the inward half – three of them on successive greens. However, he managed to contain his vexation unlike a golfer of a previous era. In *Only on Sundays* Henry Longhurst wrote affectionately of the death of Bernard Darwin:

> He has died at the age of eighty-five and, as he took to writing about golf in his early twenties and continued almost to the day of his death, there are few indeed who can remember the game without his pen and its influence in the background. Bernardo had one, to me, most amiable weakness. He allowed the game and sometimes his partners, to make him very, very cross indeed.
>
> Quite my favourite story of him concerns his start in the medal at Woking. At the first hole he laid his second shot a yard from the hole – and missed the putt. At the second he played an exquisite cut-up shot with a spoon – and missed a tiny putt for a two. At the third he missed yet another short one and was heard to be muttering darkly as he made his way to the fourth tee. There, Bernardo put his second shot two feet from the hole. In a pregnant silence he missed the putt. Brandishing his putter aloft and casting his eyes upwards to the sky, he is alleged to have cried "And now, God, perhaps You are satisfied!"*

Only on Sundays by Henry Longhurst – Cassell 1964

39

Christopher Macleod is a good example of a very fine golfer who has appeared in the final of the Moray Open on five occasions over a period of 30 years; winning it in 1959 and 1961. Apart from some 20 years in the Royal Air Force from which he retired as a Squadron Leader, he has played much of his competitive golf in Morayshire. This has been attended by a considerable amount of success and his name is inscribed on numerous tournament trophies. He is one of the very few Aberdeen students to have won the Scottish Universities' Individual Championship in 1958 when it was played for more than 30 years over the Carnoustie championship links in testing early Spring weather. As a Flying Officer he also won the Royal Air Force Championship in 1964 at his first attempt, scoring 293 after four rounds on the delightful and testing championship course at Burnham and Berrow. The runner-up was his immediate boss Squadron Leader Bill McCrea who led the Surrey County team and was a current Irish international. The fact that McCrea had, at that time, not yet won the RAF Championship may not have done much for Macleod's career prospects. Chris went on to win the RAF Championship for a second time over the same course in 1977.

A Few Holes in One

The unheralded and largely unsung winner in 1960 was the popular and genial local character 29 year-old J. Ross Anderson. In the opening rounds he had beaten two strongly fancied competitors in Hugh Stuart of Forres and the title-holder Chris Macleod, both on the 18th green. Hugh Stuart had been Scottish Boys' Champion the year before and was to become a distinguished international and Walker Cup player, and in the qualifying rounds he had equalled the course record of 68. As we have seen, Christopher Macleod was the Scottish Universities' Champion in 1958, winning the Jack Allan trophy, and in 1959 he had won a clutch of tournaments including the Moray Open. In the semi-final Anderson defeated his third scratch golfer in Farquhar Thomson at the 20th hole before beating James Shannon of Cawder, also at the 20th hole, in the final.

Ever since 1894 a sweepstake, to be described, has followed the qualifying rounds. W.G. Henderson, the club secretary, bought a ticket and drew Ross Anderson, but having so little regard for his chances he promptly sold him 'to buy a round of drinks'. Nothing daunted, the brave and confident Anderson (handicap 4) bought himself for the insignificant sum of £4-10/-, and after lifting the cup and the winner's voucher, was rewarded with a further cheque for £100 from the sweepstake. In 1968 Anderson made a handsome gesture to his golf club by donating a silver cup to be played for by the handicap qualifiers in Section 2 and since then the Ross Anderson Trophy has been awarded to the winner.

Some astonishing feats took place on one practice day for this tournament which are now recorded in the *Golfers' Handbook*.

J. Ross Anderson

Farquhar Thomson, playing in the morning in a four ball with W.J. Stewart, J.C. Thomson and David Cowper, recorded his first ace at the 15th hole. Thomson played another practice round in the evening with Ross Anderson and Billy Thomson who halved the short sixth hole in one stroke: Anderson having the second of these holes in one, his ball landing directly in the cup. The bar tills in the clubhouse must have rung merrily that night.

The Selling Sweep

This has always been a very popular and much anticipated event during the tournament week at Lossiemouth. The selling sweep consists of 16 'horses' from the scratch section of 32 players – the top 12 and four groups of 5 from the remaining highest scoring qualifiers. Raffle sweep tickets are sold prior to the start of the Open and the income starts the 'Pool'. On the Tuesday night the auction begins and the owners of the

**W. D. Campbell and Ross McConnachie, his caddie,
winner in 1951 and 2003 respectively**

first 16 raffle tickets drawn from a hat are allocated 'horses' and these are then sold to the highest bidder. The owner of a 'horse' has the option to sell or retain, but selling is uncommon and is rather frowned on. At the end of the week's match-play the 'Pool' is divided – 1/2 to the winner, ¼ to the runner-up and the balance is shared between the semi-final 'horses'.

Many competitors and their friends have interesting memories of the sweep and one such is Bill Campbell who writes from Toronto:

> In the 1951 Open my brother John, an impecunious medical student, drew me in the sweep. My elder brother bought him the other half of the ticket at the auction. I was therefore, willy nilly, elected to carry the burden of saving the family fortunes.
>
> A curious incident occurred in the second round. I was playing a chap called Jim Brodlie, a golfer with a national reputation. I had been two up after the fifteenth but all of a sudden, it seemed, I was all square on the 18th tee – Jessop's tee – which I must admit has always scared me a bit. Jim, a wily tactician, decided to play short, hoping I think that I would go out of bounds. I grasped the nettle and responded by hitting a beautiful hook over the Colonel's rock [in the grounds of *The Craig*] and right down the middle. That I thought was that: Jim could not hit the green in two. But when we came up to where my ball should have been – it was nowhere to be found!
>
> There was a fairly big crowd following the match and they all milled around on the plateau below Boyd Anderson's house. A man who had been watching the match through the club telescope, and had seen the ball land, came running down from the clubhouse. He proclaimed that the ball was: 'Richt in the middle o' the fairwye'. Nevertheless, a hundred people could not find it. It was as if someone was playing a cruel conjuring trip. The clock ticked on. My opponent sucked his teeth, remarked on the irony of fate and only checked his watch at decent intervals. Just when the five minutes was about to elapse, I heard the voice of a little quinie: 'Is this yer baw mannie?' And indeed it was my baw – nestled in a little holie – like a lintie's egg. Grass had grown over the hole which was why we couldn't see the ball. I got a lift under the rabbit scrape rule and I went on the win the hole and later the tournament. Phew! What an escape! My brother was able to complete his MB ChB in comparative affluence.
>
> We, the Canadian Campbells, later won on Alan Junor and my grandson had Ivan McKenzie as a semi-finalist. We also won the jackpot on a ticket purchased by phone from Canada with the assistance of our Lossie agent, my friend John McConachie. Our 'horse' was the incredible Norman Grant in his final (?) victory. We founded the Norman Grant Fan Club (Toronto Branch). 'Norman! Norman! He's our man! If he can't do it, No one can!' He did it too.

Bill Campbell and his mother in 1951 with the Moray, Elgin and Strathlene Trophies

My family has been very lucky in the sweep. It easily beats the Toronto Stock Market for return on investment. We, however, reject any suggestions of insider trading or game fixing by stymies or other means.

Such are the vagaries of the sweep that in 1967 Norman Grant drew and retained a 'horse' named R. J. Gray and went on to defeat him in the final.

CHAPTER FIVE
Memorable Local Winners

Norman Grant

Norman Grant of the Elgin Golf Club defeated R.M. ('Chanto') Grant of Aberdeen to win the Moray Open in 1965. The following year he became a member at Moray and embarked on a domination of the tournament which had not been seen before and may well not be equalled for many a long year. Grant has shown himself to be a master of the seaside links in all conditions and in all weathers and he has stamped his authority on many a close match with his excellent short game. His record over the past 40 years is worth looking at in some detail.

Over a period of 34 years he has reached and contested 13 finals. Between 1965 and 1980 he was the winner of five Opens and 19 years later, in 1999 at the age of 58, he carried off the crown for the 6th time – and who will say it is his last? The Moray Club championship is decided by medal play over four rounds and he has won it a record 15 times, including six in a row which ties George Thomson's record, made as long ago as 1906-11. Perhaps the zenith of his career for Norman Grant was to win the Scottish Seniors Open Amateur Championship, sponsored by *The Famous Grouse* whisky and decided by medal play, at Falkirk Tryst in the year 2000. In doing so he defeated three ex-Walker Cup players which points up the extraordinary fact that in all his playing career he did not win an international cap for Scotland. The much-capped trio were C. W. Green, J. Scott Macdonald and George Macgregor.

Some of Grant's more memorable matches were against his namesake from Aberdeen R.M. ('Chanto') Grant. When Norman won his first title in 1965 the wind was blowing a gale and he got his four at the 14th by hitting two drivers and a seven iron and sinking the putt. This was a friendly affair and he took Chanto up and down to Elgin each day in his car. In the first four day tournament at Moray in 1967 Norman Grant met an unknown quantity in R.J. Gray of Prestonfield. Gray was a Scottish Boys' and Youth internationalist who had won that year's Dalmahoy Open Amateur Championship against strong opposition.

58 year old Norman Grant – 1999

Both players were out in 34 and with an eagle and three birdies Grant ran out the winner by 3&2. A feature of the final, apart from the fine golf, was the speed with which the contestants got on with the game, taking just over two hours to play the 16 holes. R.J. Gray returned the following year and this time he won the tournament, defeating in the final Ian Rodger of Elgin who was appearing in his third final in five years.

R.M. and N.S. Grant met again in 1971 when 'Chanto' turned the tables in a match where every putt of two feet or less was conceded and took all of two hours and ten minutes to get round the Old course. Farquhar Thomson, who knows a bit about finals, having appeared in three and refereed many more, recalls that he and the gallery had difficulty keeping up with the play. In 1972, in a final thoroughly enjoyed by both players, Jocky Farquhar of Strathlene putted Grant off the golf course. Norman Grant's caddy for many years has been his friend Graham Cowper, dentist and knowledgeable golfer, who himself won the Macpherson trophy in 1982 and whose son Neal won the Ross Anderson trophy in 2002.

Farquhar Thomson

Farquhar Thomson is already a legendary figure in the annals of the Moray Golf Club. A very fine golfer, who has made 10 semi-final appearances and been three times in the final, he won the Open in 1962 defeating James Marnoch of Garmouth in the final. Moray Golf Club champion in 1964, he again reached the final where he lost to a new member in Bill Reid, the butcher from nearby Hopeman. Reid did not take up golf until he was almost thirty years of age but he worked hard at his game and taught himself to play a variety of shots. Like the very best amateurs he could hit the ball straight, or draw or fade it at will; and with a good putting

Farquhar Thomson – winner 1962

stroke he was a difficult competitor to play against. As Captain of the golf club on three occasions, 1965-67, 1977-78, and 1989-90, Farquhar Thomson has been an administrator without parallel and has steered through innovations in the running of the Open tournament and countless improvements on the golf courses. As the driving force behind the New course and its successful completion in 1979, when he was fittingly asked to declare it open by driving off the first ball, his vigour and energy have left behind a legacy for which future generations of golfers will be grateful.

Alistair Thomson

Farquhar Thomson's younger brother Alistair – professional to the Moray Golf Club for the past twenty-eight years – lived in Farquhar's shadow for some years but, in his amateur days he won the Moray Open in 1966 on the 18th green after a great battle with Ian Rodger, who had begun with a birdie three and an eagle three at the opening holes. The following year the two met again in the final of the Elgin Open Amateur and Rodger again opened with two threes and again lost on the 18th green. Alistair Thomson was to win the Moray Open twice more,

Alistair Thomson – winner 1966, 1970 and 1974

extracting the maximum of excitement from each occasion. He was a fearless match player who enjoyed single combat, and with his Arnold Palmer-like swing he was electrifying to watch and kept the galleries on their toes. In 1970 against Scottish international Alistair P. Thomson – now the professional at Inverness – he had the spectators enthralled when, with three birdies, he was four up after five holes. The Inverness golfer heightened the drama by winning the difficult short sixth with his first ever hole in one. This was a match with golf of the highest class and when the Lossiemouth Thomson won by 3&2 he needed two pars for a score of 68.

Alistair Thomson's third and last victory in 1974 was over Norman Grant in a match of old rivalries and some tension. The difficult eighteenth hole highlighted the affair. Both players hit long drives with Thomson, who was one hole up, in a deep bunker on the left of the fairway. Grant hit a beautiful second to the long plateau green and lay some twelve feet away while Thomson played one of his famous recovery shots and lay outside his opponent. He proceeded to hole a bold putt for a birdie three and win one of the more exciting finals.

H.B. Stuart

H.B. Stuart – winner in 1977 and 1978

When Hugh Stuart returned to Morayshire to live and work he re-joined the Moray Golf Club and won the Open Amateur Tournament in 1977 and 1978. This came as no great surprise as he was already a very distinguished golfer. As a pupil at Forres Academy in 1959 he won the Scottish Boys' Championship and in 1970 he was beaten by one hole by the illustrious Charlie Green in the final of the Scottish Amateur Championship at Balgownie Links. He went one better in 1972 when he beat a very fine player in A.K. (Sandy) Pirie in the final of the Scottish at Prestwick. Pirie, Green and Stuart were all Walker Cup players: the latter two being paired together in the foursomes on more than one occasion. Hugh Stuart was in the top flight of amateur golfers in his day and from 1971 he played in three successive Walker Cup matches – acquitting himself with great distinction at St Andrews in 1971 when he won all his matches against the Americans. Altogether he was capped for Scotland and Britain on 21 occasions.

Another Banker

Ian D. McIntosh, like so many bankers very economical with his figures, played much of his golf at Elgin, Moray, Banff and Royal Dornoch. At Dornoch he played with America's Ben Crenshaw and frequently partnered Brora's celebrated Jimmy Miller who, along with McIntosh, plundered many a competition in the Northern summer tournament circuit. A very experienced competitor with a game which was long and straight, McIntosh won the Moray Open in 1979 and 1988. On his way to the final in the latter year he played some golf of rare quality, not least in the quarter final where he defeated an old adversary in Norman Grant on the 18th green by holing the course in 68, one shot less than his opponent. Very many schoolmasters and fully as many bankers are excellent golfers, but as yet, there appears to be no reliable explanation to account for this phenomenon.

Ian McIntosh and Ben Crenshaw at Royal Dornoch

CHAPTER SIX
The Hat Trick Accomplished

The Eighties

The year of 1981 saw the worst weather of the tournament for many years with torrential rain at times. This did not affect the number of competitors and after the qualifying rounds 161 sponsored prizes were paid out. These were smaller prizes for eagles, birdies, longest drives or holes in one given by the sponsors as will be seen later. C.J. Macleod celebrated his return to the tournament, which he had last won 20 years earlier, by beating Farquhar Thomson in the semi-final (Thomson's 10th appearance in the semi-final stages) but losing the final to fellow member Michael Wilson. Wilson, a greenkeeper at Moray, was a phlegmatic character with a nice sense of humour. Many of his opponents did not realise that he turned off his hearing aid from tee to green to isolate himself from the noise of spectators, passing aircraft and idle chatter. Macleod at his best was a difficult man to beat but Wilson badly wanted this title to add to the Elgin and Forres crowns that he had already garnered.

In 1982 there was a record entry of 220 competitors with 32 category one golfers – players with a handicap of 5 or less – in the field. The weather was glorious all week and play began at 7 a.m. with three players going off at eight minute intervals – the last three at 5 p.m.. It was becoming obvious that the number of entrants would have to be curtailed or the New course brought in to play for the qualifying rounds. Although the weather was at its best the very demanding Moray links proved as tough as usual to master and there were numerous casualties among the better players. Michael Wilson retained the title after a good old-fashioned scrap with 'Chanto' Grant who was playing out of the Aberdeen links club Caledonian from whence he had won the title in 1971.

The 1983 tournament was won by Alistair Nichols, an Australian from Eaton Golf Club in Norwich: the first time a winner had come from south of the border since 1894. In the final Nichols defeated Norman

Grant who had figured in an extraordinary match in the second round with Gary Abel of Elgin, a strongly fancied competitor. Abel was four up with five holes to play and he could only look on in horror while his lead was whittled away until he lost the 18th hole and the match. C.E. Dick of Royal Liverpool had won the Championship as long ago as 1911 but as he had entered from Royal Dornoch where he was a member, and as he was also a Scottish international, it did not seem to count as an English victory.

Michael Wilson – winner 1981 and 1982

The following year saw the largest field ever of 237 with 44 visitors from 29 different clubs and 24 category one players, with more than £800 on offer in the form of a variety of prizes. The title this year went to Aberdeen with Jim Scott of Murcar beating Chris Macleod in the final before a gallery of more than 300 spectators. A field of 213 was entered for the 1985 contest and the qualifying cut at 155 was the lowest for years. The holder, Jim Scott and Scottish international Keith Hird, who had recently won the Cruden Bay tournament (always keenly contested by Aberdeen golfers), both missed the cut. In the final, Morty Cattanach of Garmouth defeated John McCallum by 3&2. Cattanach was the first left-handed player to win at Lossiemouth.

A Five Day Tournament

Having become a four-day Open in 1966 the most recent major change in the format of the tournament was introduced in 1986 with the decision to use both the Old and the New (opened in 1979) courses for the qualifying rounds. This change was accompanied by the extension of play to make it a five day Open and this proved so popular that fields of over 300 began to emerge. The evolution of a scoring up-date system, including outer half scores and leader boards, has been a major factor in sustaining interest in Moray Open events for many years. This became established only as a result of the enthusiasm and commitment of a number of senior members of the golf club, in particular the work over many years of the late Jimmy Campbell and the late Lachlan McIntosh.

This particular July presented the golfers with the full gamut of seaside weather including severe gales. A new star, Ivan McKenzie, headed the qualifiers with two superb rounds for a total of 145 which led the field by five shots. Another member of the Thomson family made a promising start to his career when schoolboy Kevin (son of the professional) reached the match play stages for the first time. The welcome re-appearance of some of the top Aberdeen players saw R.H. Willox of Aberdeen, playing out of Deeside, win the tournament on his debut appearance by beating the experienced Norman Grant (in his tenth final in 20 years) by 3&2. G.A. Moir of Fraserburgh continued the run of success for clubs outside of Moray by winning the following year. Moir has since gone on to pursue a highly successful career in Greenkeeping and is now the Links supervisor at St Andrews with the overall responsibility for the home of golf's seven courses. The heavy responsibility for the condition of his flagship venue, the Old Course, in the 2005 Open, rests on Moir's broad shoulders.

Present Day Format

This is now a unique event in the Scottish golfing calendar. Apart from the trophies and the considerable prize money there are prizes for competitors on each hole of the 36 hole stroke play qualifying

PRIZE STRUCTURE

MAJOR PRIZES WILL BE A COMBINATION OF VOUCHERS AND PRIZES

QUALIFYING ROUNDS

HANDICAP AGGREGATE	£65	£55	£50	£40	£35	£30
SCRATCH AGGREGATE	£65	£55	£50	£40		

MATCH PLAY

	Winner	Runner-Up	Semi-Finalists	
SCRATCH	£250	£175	£125	£125
HANDICAP 1	£200	£150	£100	£100
HANDICAP 2	£200	£150	£100	£100

■ £15 Voucher to each player eliminated in 1st Round
■ £25 Voucher to each player eliminated in 2nd Round
■ £40 Voucher to each player eliminated in 3rd Round

STABLEFORD & BOGEY COMPETITIONS

	1st	2nd	3rd	4th
HANDICAP Section 1	£40	£35	£30	£25
HANDICAP Section 2	£40	£35	£30	£25
HANDICAP Section 3	£40	£35	£30	£25

■ STABLEFORD - 34, 35, 36 Points is BUFFER ZONE
Entry Sheet Posted Tuesday at 2.00pm

■ BOGEY - 2 down, 1 down & Square is BUFFER ZONE
Entry Sheet Posted Wednesday at 2.00pm

SPECIAL PRIZES

(Qualifying Rounds Only)

■ **PAR 5's OLD & NEW** - £10 Voucher for any Eagle scored on any par 5 hole.
■ **EAGLES** - £15 Voucher for an Eagle scored on any other hole, Old or New.
■ **BERMUDA TRIANGLE** - New Course 9th, 10th & 11th.
Aggregate prizes in each of 3 handicap sections - Please add up your 'Triangle' and put it below the 'Stableford' box on your scorecard.
■ **BEST GROSS SCORE ON LAST 3 HOLES ON OLD COURSE EACH DAY BY HANDICAP 10 AND OVER** - Dinner for Two People
1629 Restaurant, Lossiemouth
■ **BEST NETT QUALIFYING SCORE BY A VISITOR TO MORAY -**
Short break accommodation sponsored by Bri-Heath B & B, Lossiemouth.
■ **SHORTIES** - Par 3's - Old Course 4th, 6th & 15th.
New Course 4th, 6th & 17th.
Aggregate prizes in each of 3 Handicap Sections. Please add your score at these holes and enter it in the "Stableford" box on your card.
■ **LONGEST DRIVES** - 18th Old & 18th New.
Special Prize for the longest drive at each of these holes each day.
(no player may win this twice)
■ **BIRDIES** - Vouchers and Golf Balls are offered for Birdies at any hole -
Please circle these.
■ **HOLE-IN-ONE** - Prizes are offered for any hole-in-one.
4th New - Prize for hole-in-one (sponsored by Harbour Treasures)
6th New - £250 for 1st hole-in-one (sponsored by Scott-Bet)
6th Old -1st hole-in-one or nearest the pin (Sponsored by Little the Jewellers)
■ **COLLECTION OF PRIZES** - Golf balls or goods/vouchers up to value of £15 from Professional. Vouchers over £15 from the Secretary.
PLEASE CIRCLE ANY BIRDIES, EAGLES etc. BEFORE HANDING IN YOUR SCORECARD.
Note: *No Competitor may win more than three sponsored prizes.*
The Tournament Committee reserves the right to alter or amend any of the conditions specified above at their sole discretion.

rounds – the prizes are donated by a variety of Elgin and Lossiemouth businesses, banks, hotels and private individuals. An example of the prizes on offer are: £10 vouchers for any eagle at a par 5 hole on the Old or New courses and £15 vouchers for an eagle at any other hole. At the six par three holes on the two courses there are aggregate prizes in all sections. The longest drives at the 18th hole of both Old and New courses attract special prizes on each qualifying day. Vouchers and golf balls are offered for birdies at any hole and numerous prizes are on offer for the Stableford and Bogey competitions which are held on the New course for those who did not qualify for the match play stages. Thousands of pounds are now available as prizes of one sort or another and the tournament is fully subscribed by the beginning of January.

Centenary Open

The centenary of the founding of the Moray Golf Club in 1989 produced a quality entry of visitors and a field of 304 competitors. Prize money of £2300 was on offer as well as the sponsors' numerous prizes in kind. In the final, Ian McGarva, Royal Air Force international and member at Moray, opened with a birdie blitz which left his Scottish international opponent Keith Hird on the ropes and McGarva ran out a comfortable winner by 5&4. McGarva had defeated a newcomer from Royal Norwich, Richard van Ree, in the quarter-final and this was a portent of things to come.

The crown went to England for only the second time in 1990 when, in glorious summer weather, Englishman Richard Van Ree of Royal Norwich returned and emerged the victor from a field of 308. He again met the very formidable Ian McGarva in the same round and this time overcame him. Van Ree survived a tight match in the semi-final where he had to win the last three holes to beat his opponent, and he defeated a very steady golfer in Mark Ballantyne by 2&1 in the final.

Mrs Betty Thomson presents the trophy to Richard Van Ree in 1990
Others are S. Simpson, W.F. Thomson and Dr D.J.C. Cameron

54

A McGarva Encore

Ian McGarva was a large relaxed man with an excellent game and the sort of delicate touch big men often have on and around the greens. In the match play games he was involved in at Moray he was always attended by an aura of excitement – anything might happen. In the 1991 final against Bill Bryce of East Kilbride he was one down and two to play with his opponent on the front edge of the green at the long and dangerous 17th hole. McGarva's second shot was pulled into the marram grass of the high dunes on the left of the fairway and apparently lost. The ball was found with the aid of the attendant crowd and duly hacked out. Bryce three putted and the hole was halved in the par of five. The 18th hole was won by McGarva and the match was now all square, and they set off down the 19th attended by an excited crowd of spectators. Bryce played the hole well and got a birdie 3 but McGarva drilled a chip shot into the cup for an unlikely half and won the game at the 20th hole. His opponent was left contemplating what might have been.

The Hat Trick

Competition was always so intense and the Old course so unrelenting that it seemed that the dream of three victories in a row would never be realised. But history was made when Ivan McKenzie from nearby Burghead wore the victor's laurels for a record three years in succession in 1994 – and appropriately enough the feat was accomplished on the hundredth anniversary of the founding of the Northern Amateur Championship. McKenzie set the bar at a height which is unlikely to be bettered for a long time, and in doing so he revealed that earlier in the year his expectation of playing, let alone completing the hat trick, had almost been ruined by ill-health – 'but things improved'.

McKenzie, a modest 47-year old, was a late starter who did not take up golf until he was well into his twenties and the irregular hours of his occupation in the maltings industry prevented him getting as much competitive golf as his rivals. Like so many good golfers his build is of medium height with powerful shoulders and arms and he is blessed with an admirably compact swing and an apparently serene temperament. Very powerful and accurate off the tee he is a good iron player and a good putter with a smooth stroke, and an even better putter when under pressure. Club champion in 1988, he has played a leading role in numerous Moray golf club team successes and has two Northern Counties Cup victories under his belt.

In his first victory in 1992 McKenzie beat a renowned competitor in R.J. (Robbie) Sheils in the final. He may well have been said to have snatched victory from the jaws of defeat on this occasion as the unfortunate Sheils was one up after 17 holes but three putted the 18th and drove into the buckthorn to lose the match at the first extra hole.

There was a capacity field for this event with 348 entered and playing, including visitors from 53 other clubs. The holder, the powerful Ian McGarva, was in the field with the fancied Donald Jamieson from Aberdeen, and the ever-green Norman Grant led the qualifiers with a splendid 143 total.

A Champagne Year

1993 was another excellent year. A very large field with many visitors including golfers from Dubai, Canada and Pakistan demonstrated how air travel is shrinking the world. Ian McGarva led the qualifiers with 139 – 70, 69, and 14-year old Gary Thomson, son of the professional, qualified comfortably with 151, including a 74 on the Old course. Youth had its fling in the match play stages when young Gary put down a marker by beating Robin Caldow of Milnathorpe by 3&2 and the young Alan Junor of Forres beat the very experienced Norman Grant by 5&3. Junor went on to defeat the redoubtable McGarva in the semi-final while McKenzie was struggling to cope with another young pretender in Malcolm Macleman. This was a heroic encounter in which no quarter was asked or given and the protagonists shared an eagle and seven birdies in the first 16 holes; the last birdie at the 16th falling to McKenzie who became one up and just held on to win. In an enthralling final Junor was three holes to the good at one stage but an unruffled Ivan was 2 up after 12 and won by 3&2.

However, the real icing on the cake this year was reserved for Graham Thomson, a hard working fishing skipper, who, taking his annual break, holed his tee shot at the 158 yard 11th hole on the New course in the qualifying rounds and collected the sponsor's prize of a case of champagne. Fittingly enough the sponsor at this hole was the well-known 'North's Leading Bookmaker – Scotscoup the Bookies' of Elgin.

The Third Title

Ivan McKenzie extracted the utmost drama from his third successive victory in the Moray Open of 1994 by producing a series of desperate finishes. In the semi-final he met a confident Robbie Sheils who had just underlined his considerable talent by winning the Elgin Open the week before. This was a memorable encounter and deserves describing in some detail. According to a gracious Sheils; 'Funnily enough one of the abiding memories of the Moray Open for me is not about any of my wins, but

Ivan McKenzie – 1994

56

of being beaten in this semi-final by Ivan who produced some of the most inspired putting I have ever seen.' Sheils was three up after six holes, the wind began to blow and Ivan began to claw his way back, and the match was level at the 14th hole.

Then began a quite extraordinary train of events. Ivan single putted the 15th, 16th, 17th and 18th holes to remain all square. They set off again down the 19th without any sign of McKenzie's gifted putter cooling down. He single putted that hole *and* the 20th *and* the 21st to stay in the game and, – just to rub salt into the wound – he played an awkward bunker shot with one knee on the grass at the 22nd hole and single putted to win. And after all that, he went out in the afternoon to win the final. As Sheils so correctly said 'It brought home the old golf adage that "it's not how, but how many".'

The 'shoot-out' with Sheils delayed the final and tested McKenzie's temperament to the full, but his chance had come and he did not mean to waste it. For the second successive year he found himself facing Alan Junor, whose home course was now Royal Dornoch, and eventually, in a very close match in which some excellent putts were holed, Ivan emerged triumphant in front of the large crowd awaiting him at the 18th green.

Fittingly, at the prize-giving which, by long-standing tradition, is conducted on the 18th green below the multitude of spectators, the handsome silver cup was presented to him by Mrs Winnie Peterkin Campbell. Her husband, W.D. (Bill) Campbell had once more returned to play in the tournament which he had first graced with his presence by winning it as long ago as 1948. Bill made his usual humorous and self-deprecating speech remembering times long past and comparing the golfers of his day to the young giants of today.

Ian Geddes

The next year might have proved an anti-climax but now some very good young players were eager to make their mark. Ian Geddes of the Hopeman club had been a regular entrant in the Moray Open for a number of years and was keen to emulate the last Hopeman player to find his way to the winner's rostrum 31 years previously. He entered the tournament with a very orderly short game and putting particularly well – always an asset on an unforgiving seaside links. Playing confidently he met Philip McPherson, another good Hopeman man, in the quarter finals and found himself with two putts from a distance for the match on the 18th green. His first putt lay two feet from the hole and then a nervous yip saw the match off down the 19th. With his opponent comfortably on in two Geddes had now recovered enough composure to sink a tramline putt for an unlikely birdie three and the match.

In the semi-final he met an opponent of unrivalled experience in

Norman Grant and he was duly four down after 9 holes. Playing steadily he reduced the deficit with two birdies in the inward half and they faced the dreaded 18th all square. With Norman set for a solid four, Ian was 20 feet away at the back of the green and feeling that he must not three putt. However, to his relief he holed it, and he was in his first Moray Open final.

The final against Alan Duncan was played in a strong wind and the golf was a little ragged. On the long 8th hole Geddes was faced with a downhill putt of about five feet for a half when he had his Joyce Wethered moment. Glancing at the horizon he saw two jet aircraft coming in to land. He went through his usual preparation and by the time he struck the ball a jet was thundering over his head. 'What *are* you doing,' said a friend, 'didn't you hear the jets?' 'What jets?' came the reply, followed by a wink. Geddes was putting so well he was confident that he wouldn't miss. One up on the 18th tee with a left to right wind blowing, Ian cut his tee shot and, with the sort

Ian Geddes receives the Cup from
Mrs Colin McConnachie

of luck rarely experienced on that infamous hole, his drive hit the out of bounds wall and finished safely on the fairway. His next shot finished 18 inches from the hole and he had won the Moray Open.

The Wethered story is variously told of St Andrews, Troon and Sheringham where Miss Wethered was putting on the 17th green in one of her many championships. A passing train puffed and snorted loudly as she putted. On being congratulated on her imperturbability she is alleged to have asked, 'What train?'

CHAPTER SEVEN
A New Generation Arrives

Robert J. (Robbie) Sheils

A very good strong golfer equipped with an excellent temperament and a sound method which could make the game look easy, now appeared on the local, and the national, scene. Robert Sheils had already confirmed his great ability by winning the Elgin Open in 1994 and had been beaten by Ivan McKenzie in the 1994 Moray semi-final which has been described above. He further confirmed his status as a golfer of the first rank by reaching the last eight in the British Amateur Championship of 1994 which was held at Nairn Golf Club and won by Lee James of Dorset.

Robbie Sheils receives the trophy from John Campbell, a Lossiemouth man
and ex professional at Royal Aberdeen Golf Club

Having played second fiddle to Ivan in the 1992 final, Robbie was keener than ever to have his name inscribed on the old cup, and this he accomplished in 1996. In the final against the young David Main he was all square after six holes. At the seventh he hit a drive and a three wood and holed the putt for a birdie. From there he won the next four holes and went on to win by 5&4. The low handicap section that year was won by the late Donald Rattray, a well-known local artist whose paintings are much sought after. The three previous winners of the Moray Open had been given one of Rattray's signed paintings and Sheils was looking forward to receiving the much prized Rattray painting of the Old Course. To his great disappointment he was presented with the cup, a voucher and a barometer. Sheils retained the title in 1997, winning the final by 3&2 over Norman Grant - the golfer whose name runs like a thread through the latter part of this narrative.

The New Millennium

In 1900 the Championship was won by J. Ogilvie Kemp and in the following 30 years eight more Mortonhall players would appear in the final at Moray. But times change and Mortonhall golfers no longer travel to Lossiemouth to compete. The millennium year of 2000 witnessed a very fine display of golf between two outstanding local men in Sheils and Gary Thomson in the final. After eight holes Sheils was three down and in his own picturesque phrase he 'thought his goose was cooked'. Like the excellent match player he is, he then turned up the heat and birdied the 9th, 10th and 11th holes in quick succession. With a birdie two at the 15th and his opponent three putting the 16th he felt that with a two hole advantage he was home and dry. But to quote him again 'it's never over till the fat lady sings', and Gary had a surprise in store. At the long 17th (509 yards) into the wind Thomson hit a beautiful second shot 'off the deck' with a driver 270 yards into the heart of the green, and lay some 20 feet from the pin. Sheils played a three wood and blocked it to the right of the green, leaving himself with an almost impossible shot to a flag which was placed only three feet or so from the right edge. However, he played a pitch and run to 15 feet, and, after Gary had failed with his eagle putt, Robbie manfully holed his putt to win his third Moray Open.

The Search For Length

The latest technology being used in the production of golf clubs – and, according to Jack Nicklaus, golf balls in particular – is said to be having an effect on the game by producing lower and lower scores, and courses are having to be lengthened as a result. The alchemy of the Greenkeeper with his more and more sophisticated techniques and machinery may also have an influence on scoring. Fifty years ago the Moray links had many more gorse bushes, more rough and narrower fairways, whereas today the whins have been cut back, the fairways are wider and in parts the rough is more or less non-existent. Importantly, the greens are commonly beautifully manicured which leads to lower scores. Although scoring has improved, one has to remember that almost a century has elapsed since Tom Fernie holed the Old course in competition in 65 strokes. There is no point in hitting a drive 300 yards or more if the ball finishes in a gorse bush; but until a club is invented which will hit the ball straight, length alone will not lower scores. The scurrilous cartoon which appeared in *Golfing* about the turn of the last century depicting the Lossiemouth greenkeeper, with his rake and barrow beside him, sitting smoking his pipe, attracted much comment and many letters to the editor. Whatever the truth of it then, the excellent Greenkeeping staff today travel about the courses in their four wheel buggies and work together as a team.

A Lossiemouth greenkeeper at work

The professional game has had an effect on the amateur game with players being more and more deliberate, and a competitive round today can take four hours or more, whereas in the first Northern Championship in 1894 two rounds with lunch in between took all of five hours.

Gary Thomson

A new tournament record was set in 1997 when Gary Thomson led the field with a total of 132 – 65, 67. On the New course he came close to starting with three bogeys but his putter saved him on each green and a good birdie two at the 4th hole established his rhythm. From then on he played steadily and a fine finish of three successive birdies saw him post a four under par 65. His inspiration stayed with him on the following day on the Old course and he shot a fine 67, again four under par. The figures for this round are worth setting out:

Out 3,4,5,2,3,3,3,5,3   31   In 4,3,4,5,5,3,3,5,4 36.

1998 was the year when 19-year old Gary, the younger son of the Moray Golf Club's long-standing professional Alistair Thomson, set out to emulate his father who, as we have seen, won the title on three occasions as an amateur. When he reached the semi-final stage Gary met a fine golfer in Stephen Leith and found himself one down playing the

Gary Thomson – twice winner of the Moray Open

tough 18th hole. A well-played approach shot to the high plateau green before the usual daunting crowd of spectators saw the hole won with a birdie three and the combatants set off down the 19th. The first hole at Moray is eminently birdie-able from the fairway and with Leith down the middle and Thomson lodged on Mount Lebanon on the left anything might happen. Leith played a delicate little shot to a few feet from the flag but from an awkward lie his opponent put his approach inches from the pin. Leith missed his putt and lost the match to a second successive birdie. In the other semi-final Norman Grant defeated the three in a row winner, Ivan McKenzie, by the handsome margin of 6&5.

The final – if not youth versus beauty – was certainly rookie versus old campaigner. The legendary 57-year old Norman Grant is the only player to have won the Moray Open and the Elgin Open in the same year and he has done it twice – in 1969 and 1980 – more or less before his young opponent had seen the light of day. Norman was now playing in his 11th final, having already won the title five times, and the young Thomson was in no doubt as to the difficulty of his task. The skies were suitably overcast as if the golf might produce thunder and lightning. The match was a dingdong affair and Gary was surprised to find himself three up with five holes to play. As he has so often done, Norman drew on his vast experience of this seaside links and was but one down playing the 18th hole. Playing first Grant struck a fine approach shot to the plateau green and put the pressure firmly on his opponent.

In response the young man got his ball safely on the putting surface some 30 feet beyond the pin. With the wind blowing fiercely, and the expectant crowd filling the natural amphitheatre behind the green, in his own words - 'I hit my long putt just hoping to lay it close to the hole, and to my, and everyone else's surprise, it went straight in and I had captured the Moray Open title'. A huge cheer went up, Norman shook his hand, and we had witnessed the advent of a new talent.

A codicil must be added to the author's statement about Norman Grant. It has now been ascertained that, in 1951, W.D. (Bill) Campbell, in three consecutive weeks, acquired the Moray, Elgin and Strathlene trophies, and that he also added the Elgin Club Championship for good measure.

In 1998 Gary Thomson had taken up a golfing scholarship in the United States at Charleston Southern University in Southern Carolina, but he returned on holiday in 1999 to defend the title he had won in such exciting circumstances. This year there were 336 players with a waiting list of 100 hoping for a place in the field. Many golf clubs were represented with visitors from as far afield as Germany, the USA, Canada and Australia. The organising committee coped with the numbers by sending off the competitors in threes at ten minute intervals from 7a.m. to 5p.m. on both Old and New courses.

This, however, was to be Norman Grant's year. In the second round he met and defeated Kevin Thomson followed by the persistent Ivan McKenzie in the semi-final. The final against a comparative youngster in Stephen Leith was played in a stiff wind. Anyone who knows the Lossie links will understand how strong the wind was when Grant required a four iron for his second at the 1st hole and two woods and a hole-high pitch to reach the 11th green – but twenty feet away – where he holed the putt for his par to square the match. From then on he won the 12th with a birdie to go one up, halved the 13th in par figures, took the 14th into the wind with a par figure, and as he so often does, he birdied the 16th to win by 3&2. And so, the oldest golfer ever to win the Lossiemouth tournament at the age of fifty-eight, had captured his sixth Moray Open title.

The Young Thomsons

A remarkable match took place in 2002 when the two brothers Gary and Kevin Thomson, contested the final. The match coincided with their father's 25 years as professional to the Moray Golf Club and, regardless of who emerged as the winner, this would be a very special day for the Thomson family. The match was one of high quality and the 9th and 10th holes proved decisive for the outcome. Kevin birdied both holes to find himself a further hole adrift as Gary also had a birdie at the 9th and then holed his approach shot for an eagle two at the 10th. After they had both driven at the 12th hole Kevin casually asked his brother if he realised that he, Gary, was four under par for the eleven holes played. Until that point Gary's intense concentration on the match was such that thoughts of his score had not entered his head. Perhaps this is what present day golf psychologists refer to as 'being in the zone'. Each player had one bogey in the round and although Kevin pitched and putted well to secure some fighting halves, his younger brother triumphed by 3&2. It may well be that Gary Thomson's stringency with figures on the golf course perhaps owes something to the fact that he holds a first class honours degree in mathematics from the University of St Andrews.

Ross McConnachie

Another new talent emerged in 2003 with the advent of nineteen year-old Ross McConnachie who, as a fourteen-year old, had already established a record for the Moray Open when he became the youngest ever player to contest a final. Ross, playing in his first Moray Open, was beaten in the final of the low handicap section by Mark Richford. Having acquired a taste for competitive golf at the highest level Ross set about sharpening his game by continual practice; paying particular attention to his short game.

He began the week in a cheerful frame of mind as he was playing good steady golf, but with no thought of winning the tournament. However, two steady qualifying rounds of 72 and 74 confirmed the soundness of his game and increased his confidence, as he felt comfortable in match play situations. With steady golf he won his first round against Jeff Kelly but wobbled somewhat in the next match against Chris Stuart. Three down after 10 holes he rallied strongly and won on the 18th green against an opponent who was to win the Club Championship the following year. Against Ronnie Dunbar in the quarter-final he met an opponent who had won his first two matches at the 20th – this match again went to the 20th, but on this occasion Ross ran out the winner.

As his driver had been letting him down, he went to the practice ground on the Friday morning and hit a bag of balls with it. Nevertheless, as he had done all week, he continued to drive with his three wood in his semi-final against former finalist Bill Bryce, and won by 5&4 without losing a hole.

In the final McConnachie found himself pitted against the form horse in Gary Thomson, but he remembered that he had beaten Gary by one hole in the first round of the 2001 contest. Two down after two holes he said to his caddy (who was a sound choice: his father) – 'Uh Uh, this could go horribly wrong' – particularly as he thought he could see some spectators leaving. However, to his relief he steadied himself with a par and a birdie but remained two down. He now began to feel more relaxed and enjoy the experience, and even exchanged some banter with the usual large number of spectators – 300 or more – who follow Moray Open finals. Thirteen straight pars followed with the aid of some 'backs-to-the-wall' putting and the young gladiators arrived at the 18th hole all square.

Gary was safely on the plateau green in two and Ross was below the bank on the right faced with a horrible shot. Taking out his lob wedge he played a blind, miraculous shot a la Mickelson – it has been called a 'parachute shot' which describes it exactly- as the ball landed softly five feet from the hole. The astonished gallery applauded and the hole was halved in four. Let the winner describe the 19th hole.

Ross McConnachie 2003 winner

'On the 19th I asked my dad for my driver which he gave me reluctantly. I consciously swung slowly and hit a good drive and found the green. Gary's drive was left and he was still some way from the hole in two. I left my first putt 6 feet short and Gary holed out in 4. I was left with a straight uphill putt and thought of all the hours spent practising for this moment. I composed myself and hit the putt confidently and watched it into the hole. It was a great feeling.'

Ross had to compose himself again to deliver the winner's acceptance speech at the traditional site on the 18th green before the usual large crowd of spectators, friends and families gathered in the natural amphitheatre in front of the old stone clubhouse as has happened ever since the first Championship so long ago in 1894.

Brian Fotheringham

Another young golfing talent has emerged in the last four years in the form of Brian Fotheringham of Forres, who ran out the winner in 2001. Brian's desire to play in the Moray Open had been whetted by caddying for his friend Alan Junor of Royal Dornoch in Junor's two epic final matches against Ivan McKenzie in the last two of the 'hat trick' years. The organisation of the tournament by the Club, with the scorers on the course, and the big score boards, constantly updated, made him anxious to relish the experience for himself. His introduction to the qualifying

Brian Fotheringham
Winner in 2001 and 2004

rounds could scarcely have been bettered when he accomplished a rare feat in playing the 36 holes of the Old and New courses in level par, with but one bogey and one birdie in the two rounds.

On the Wednesday and Thursday he twice had to go to the 19th to win his matches and he encountered an experienced opponent in Philip McPherson of Hopeman in Friday morning's semi-final. When they stood on the 16th tee McPherson was two up with three to play, and when he hit a beautiful second to within 10 feet of the stick it looked all over bar the shouting – particularly as Fotheringham had struck a wild tee shot 60 yards off line and almost on to the beach. A helpful spectator found the ball and somehow Fotheringham scrambled a half in par. He then eagled the long 17th and sank a 25 foot plus putt for a birdie at the 18th to take the match into extra time. Almost inevitably he produced another birdie at the 19th to win what had seemed like an irretrievably lost cause. After a nervous start to the afternoon final he pulled himself together and defeated David Baker of Crewe by 4&3.

In the 2004 contest the young tigers of the links fought it out amongst themselves In Thursday's quarter-finals Fotheringham met the holder Ross McConnachie, and after being three up the match was square by the 18th tee. Here Brian was in a fairway bunker and could only move the ball some 40 yards, but he then pitched to 25 feet and holed the putt. The match went to the 20th before he took on Gary Thomson in the final. For a long way there was little to choose between them until at the long 17th Thomson almost holed a 40 yard bunker shot to square the match. The 18th and three extra holes were halved until at the 4th – a long par three – Brian holed a 20 foot birdie putt and closed out an excellent match.

CHAPTER EIGHT
One Hundred Years of Serious Fun

There has always been a lighter side to the golf championships at Lossiemouth – it has not all been about winning trophies. When the Stotfield and Marine Hotels were built there was much socialising among the visitors and the golf club members. Competitions of teams of married men versus single men, visitors versus members and mixed foursomes were popular each year, and were followed by dinner and dancing in the Stotfield Hotel. Women's dress proved a major practical obstacle to their moves onto the links where the wearing of a hat prevented a full golf swing and was impossible in the wind, of which

A mixed foursome on the 18th Green – with caddies in 1903

there was no shortage at Lossie. Hamilton describes how women were laced into stiff corsets, splinted with vertical pieces of whalebone and pulled tight when dressing in the morning. The first serious women golfers soon equipped themselves with an elasticated cummerbund, worn in reserve round the waist and called the 'Miss Higgins', which was slipped down to below knee level, controlling the skirt, when playing in the wind.*

According to *The Bulger*, in the early days, concerts were held in Lossiemouth Town Hall in which the talented visitors played a major part, but they did not seem to attract much local support. The golf club had a long-standing friendly relationship with the Senior Service, and officers of the Fleet whose ships were at Invergordon, or in the vicinity of Lossiemouth in the Moray Firth, were made honorary members of the club. Visits to the Fleet were organised for club members, and the officers of the Second Cruiser Squadron presented the club with a handsome telescope in 1910, and in 1925 the officers of *H.M.S. Vindictive* gave an aerial photograph of the course to the club. Up until the second war it was common to see gentlemen in stiff shirts with dinner jacket and black tie, accompanied by their ladies in long dresses, stroll over to the Moray Golf Club on a summer evening after dinner in the Stotfield or Marine Hotels. But the club has long discontinued the purchase of champagne, kummel, crème de menthe and other exotic liqueurs which might have been drunk in these days, although there is still a plentiful supply of claret, beers and the club's own excellent malt whisky.

> # Moray Golf Club.
>
> For the " At Home " on board H.M.S. Shannon, on Monday, 29th August.
>
> Hon. Secy
>
> ———
>
> *Boats will be at Lossiemouth Harbour from 3-30 to 4.*

As at St Andrews there was no golf on a Sunday at Lossiemouth and the courses had a well-earned rest. Many members were accustomed to London clubs where they could while away Sunday afternoons without

---

Golf – Scotland's Game by David Hamilton at The Partick Press (1998)

the distraction of wife or family, and repeated requests were made to the Council for the opening of the smoking-room of the clubhouse on Sundays. Eventually, in 1923, twelve London members, headed by Walter Shakespeare and Lewis Noad, sent the following letter to the secretary:

Dear Sir,

We, the undersigned members, request that the lounge of the clubhouse be opened on Sundays during August and the half of September from 2 p.m. until 7 p.m. for the use of members only – lady members and visitors not to be admitted. It is understood that no refreshments of any description are to be served.

As on previous occasions the Council was of the opinion that the granting of the request was *ultra vires*, and that those members who were bored by six weeks of Sunday afternoons in Lossiemouth had no other course than to lump it. However, after a little more discreetly applied pressure, the matter was duly brought up at the next annual general meeting in the form of a motion which won the necessary support, and the clubhouse was opened on Sundays the following year. No doubt the matter of refreshments was readily solved with a little ingenuity.

In the past 50 odd years the socialising has continued and many golfers, with or without their families, have taken to spending a week's holiday in Lossie at tournament time. Golf clubs such as Holland Bush, Littlestone, Lutterworth and Royal Norwich have provided a regular cadre of competitors for many years and the last three continue to do so. Well-known characters like Douglas Dempster, a past captain of Royal Aberdeen golf club, visited Lossiemouth and played in the tournament for more than 50 years, and the caravan in which he stayed was frequently a dropping-off point for golfers seeking refreshment while playing the New course. Graham Millar, London stockbroker and *bon viveur*, accompanied by many friends, was a regular visitor who won the Ross

R. M. Grant ('Chanto')
Winner in 1971 and 1976

Anderson trophy in 1980 and enjoyed some success in fishing the river with 'Chanto' Grant and Arthur McKerron. The fishing was exciting and great fun for the participants, but the fishers may not always have had permission, and perhaps it was not always carried out by entirely legal means. One occasional visitor to the tournament, participating in one of those nightly trips, was heard to exclaim, 'Good God, he's a client of mine', when told the name of the owner of the river.

Douglas Dempster and Ian Ritchie led a syndicate of competitors which did very well in the selling sweep for many years, and McKerron also landed the occasional interesting touch in the auction. After the excitement of the final the Friday night buffet and dance in the old clubhouse is a gathering of old and new friends year on year which makes the tournament so memorable.

Let David Brooks, past captain of Royal Norwich Golf Club and competitor at Moray for 35 years, have the last word.

> The Norwich connection has three separate strands. Firstly, having been a full, rather than a service member of the Moray Golf Club during my time in the Fleet Air Arm at *H.M.S. Fulmar* I had very happy memories of the whole experience. Having left the Navy, settled in Norwich and joined Royal Norwich, I headed North annually on holiday with my family to compete at Lossie and Elgin in Open weeks. This was in the days before the opening of the New course at Moray and the subsequent expansion of the Moray Open into the massive event it is today. We have made minor ripples on the surface of success at Moray. In the early years qualifying in the scratch to enjoy early exits and the pleasures of the consolations, playing with old friends, after a little mild alcoholic preparation. I recall losing the final of the Macpherson Rose Bowl to Albert McKenzie of Hopeman, whose son Albert later turned professional, and more recently defeat in the semi-final in 2003.

> The second strand was the nice present of the victory of Richard Van Ree in 1990 when my duties as Captain at Royal Norwich prevented me from travelling. Sadly he injured his neck and was lost to golf for many years. An interesting man, he was a dentist when he won; grew disillusioned with dentistry, qualified as an accountant at which he also became successful, but eventually returned to his roots as a 'Fang Farrier' as the navy would have called him. The third Norwich strand comes through Alan Nichols who entered almost by accident while holidaying with his family near Nairn. His son Andrew, a keen and later successful Norfolk golfer, heard of the Open and entered and his Dad entered too to keep him company. He was unable to defend the title in 1984 so I had the privilege of carrying the trophy back to Moray, the nearest I ever got to it!

A few memories from years past. In 1971 I caddied for 'Chanto' Grant. In the quarter-final, playing Ian Rodger, he holed his tee shot at the 4th hole – the hole being cut behind the mound on the right. That evening, Chanto, a keen fisherman, whose nocturnal habits in the company of Arthur McKerron were well known, elected to leave his clubs and shoes in the boot of my car ready for the semi-final. As tee time approached on the Friday morning there was no sign of Chanto, until, with disqualification looming, a van appeared down the beach road beside the first tee. Chanto, not looking too well, disembarked. Climbing on to the tee, he changed his shoes and proceeded to smack one down the middle. At the 4th hole the pin was again behind the shoulder. Chanto hit the same easy cut some 200 yards into the green; the ball came to rest on the plugged hole from the previous day, the pin having been moved a few feet! What a golfer! No one could persuade a driver [affectionately called 'Jezebel'] into the air off those tight lies like Chanto Grant. He was not overlong but very straight and never rattled. In the final, played in a dense and swirling haar, he just overcame his namesake N.S. Grant.

With the massive fields these days, hugely oversubscribed by both members and visitors, the tournament is a testament to the organisational talents of the Moray Golf Club. As a result of its very success the tournament appears to this ageing golfer to have lost a little of its old intimacy and warmth. This is not a complaint, because having played in it for 35 years there are always a few folk in the clubhouse bar for me to sit down with. But the newer breed will have their own friends and cannot experience the old days of companionship and fun with the like of Douglas Dempster, Glen McKay, Norman Grant, Bill Reid, Jimmy Marnoch, Wattie Wilken, Bob Calder, Ian Wilson and many others. I am very pleased I didn't miss them.

It was, from the start, and still is, serious fun.

APPENDIX
The Moray Open Amateur Tournament instituted in 1894

WINNERS

1894 L.W. Macpherson (Baberton)
1895 A.J.T. Allan (Watsonians)
1896 J. McCulloch (Aberdeen)
1897 L.W. Macpherson (Baberton)
1898 L.W. Macpherson (Baberton)
1899 J.W. Wharton Duff (The Hon. Company)
1900 J. Ogilvie Kemp (Mortonhall)
1901 W.D. Davidson (Aberdeen)
1902 J.J. Gillespie (Mortonhall)
1903 J.Gordon Simpson (St. Andrews University)
1904 Robert Harris (Carnoustie)
1905 Clive Lawrence (Nairn)
1906 F.H.Scroggie (Carnoustie)
1907 Gordon Lockhart (Prest. St. Nicholas)
1908 Gordon Lockhart (Prest. St. Nicholas)

RUNNERS-UP

John Sutherland (Royal Dornoch)
L.W. Macpherson (Baberton)
Duncan MacLaren (Mortonhall)
Duncan MacLaren (Mortonhall
A. Cooper (Aberdeen Victoria)
J.G. Stewart (Carnoustie)
I.C. MacGregor (Nairn)
A.G. Thomson (Edinburgh Academicals)
J.H. Peebles (Clifton Downs}
J.A. Donaldson (Aberdeen Bon-Accord)
Captain A. Chalmers (Royal Aberdeen)
C.A. Macpherson (Mortonhall)
W.C. White (Lundin Links)
R. Gelletly, Jnr. (Greenhill)
Dr. Marshall (Hamilton)

WINNERS	RUNNERS-UP
1909 Donald Grant (Royal Dornoch)	Lieut. W.D. Allan (Moray)
1910 Ian Munro (Strathpeffer)	Donald Grant (Royal Dornoch)
1911 C.E. Dick (Royal Dornoch)	G.R. Thomson (Moray)
1912 A. Guthrie Harvey (Nairn)	H. Kingsley Brown (Mortonhall)
1913 G.R. Thomson (Moray)	A. Cooper, Jnr. (Deeside)
1914 G.C. Manford (Edinburgh University)	W.C. White (Mortonhall)
1915–1919 *(No Tournament during the War years)*	
1920 Capt. Kynoch Cumming (Moray)	A.G. Campbell (Moray)
1921 G.C. Manford (Luffness New)	G.R. Thomson (Moray)
1922 G.C. Manford (Luffness New)	G. Seymour Noon (Didsbury)
1923 W.C. White (Mortonhall)	T.H. Osgood (Forres)
1924 A.G. Campbell (Moray)	W. Willis Mackenzie (Mortonhall)
1925 J.T. Bookless (Inverness)	J.G. Rowan (Drumpellier)
1926 J.G. Rowan (Drumpellier)	Neil Paterson (Moray and Sandy Lodge)
1927 John Birnie, Jnr (Inverness)	J.L. Laing (Moray)
1928 R. Stirling (Bishopbriggs)	L.B. Sanderson (Inverness)
1929 George Wilson (Nairn)	P.F. Cameron (Forres)
1930 Hugo Ronald (Moray)	George Wilson (Nairn)
1931 H. McMaster (Old Ranfurly)	A. McKenzie (Moray)
1932 R. Falconer (Moray)	W. Donaldson (New Galloway)
1933 R.S. Walker (Aberdeen University)	Donald Cameron (Kirkintilloch)
1934 Dr. J.C. Jessop (Moray)	J.G. Royan (Hayston)
1935 R.S. Walker (Deeside)	Donald Cameron (Kirkintilloch)
1936 Dr. J.C. Jessop (Moray)	D.C. Leith Buchanan (Nairn)
1937 R.S. Walker (Deeside)	H.G. Macintosh (Royal Aberdeen)
1938 K.B. Murray (Eastwood)	J.S. Montgomerie (Cambuslang)
1939 Dr. J.C. Jessop (Moray)	A.M.W. Coburn (Aberdeen University)
1940–1946 *(No Tournament during the War years)*	
1947 G.T. Murray (Moray)	A.J.D. Blaikie (Royal Musselburgh)
1948 W.D. Campbell (Moray)	B.W. Wilken (Elgin)
1949 Dr. J.C. Jessop (Moray)	A. Kinnaird (Moray)
1950 J. Paterson (Spey Bay)	G.T. Murray (Moray)
1951 W.D. Campbell (Moray)	Dr. H.N.M. Thomson (Elgin)
1952 A. Cordiner (Murcar)	J. Lindsay (Falkirk Tryst)
1953 J. Lindsay (Falkirk Tryst)	I.P.A. Rodger (Moray)
1954 D.F. Beatson (Kingsknowe)	C.J. Macleod (Moray)
1955 J. Paterson (Buckpool)	E.B. Robinson (Moray)
1956 E.B. Robinson (Moray)	W.J. Stewart (Moray)
1957 W. Hector (Buckpool)	A.S.E. Dale (Baberton)
1958 A.W. How (Moray)	W. Hector (Buckpool)
1959 C.J. Macleod (Moray)	S.F. Smith (Moray)
1960 J. Ross Anderson (Moray)	J. Shannon (Cawder)
1961 C.J. Macleod (Moray)	R.M. Grant (Elgin)
1962 W.F. Thomson (Moray)	J. Marnoch (Garmouth)
1963 I.P.A. Rodger (Elgin)	J. Morrison (Moray)
1964 W. Reid (Moray)	W.F. Thomson (Moray)
1965 N.S. Grant (Elgin)	R.M. Grant (Hazelhead)
1966 A. Thomson (Moray)	I.P.A. Rodger (Moray)
1967 N.S. Grant (Elgin)	R.J. Gray (Prestonfield)
1968 R.J. Gray (Prestonfield)	I.P.A. Rodger (Elgin)
1969 N.S. Grant (Moray)	W.F. Thomson (Moray)

1970 A. Thomson (Moray)
1971 R.M. Grant (Aberdeen Caledonian)
1972 J. Farquhar (Strathlene)
1973 N.S. Grant (Moray)
1974 A. Thomson (Moray)
1975 I.G. Taylor (Moray)
1976 R.M. Grant (Aberdeen Caledonian)
1977 H.B. Stuart (Moray)
1978 H.B. Stuart (Moray)
1979 I.D. Mackintosh (Moray)
1980 N.S. Grant (Moray)
1981 M. Wilson (Moray)
1982 M. Wilson (Moray)
1983 A.D. Nichols (Eaton)
1984 J.A. Scott (Murcar)
1985 M. Cattanach (Garmouth)
1986 R.H. Willox (Deeside)
1987 G.A. Moir (Fraserburgh)
1988 I.D. McIntosh (Moray)
1989 I. McGarva (Moray)
1990 R. Van Ree (Royal Norwich))
1991 I. McGarva (Moray)
1992 I.J. McKenzie (Moray)
1993 I.J. McKenzie (Moray)
1994 I.J. McKenzie (Moray)
1995 I.S. Geddes (Hopeman)
1996 R.J. Sheils (Moray)
1997 R.J. Sheils (Moray)
1998 G. Thomson (Moray)
1999 N.S. Grant (Moray)
2000 R.J. Sheils (Moray)
2001 B. Fotheringham (Forres)
2002 G. Thomson (Moray)
2003 R. McConnachie (Moray)
2004 B. Fotheringham (Forres)
2005

A.P. Thomson (Inverness)
N.S. Grant (Moray)
N.S. Grant (Moray)
P.G. Buchanan (Williamwood)
N.S. Grant (Moray)
B. Pennington (Moray)
I. Imray (Moray)
B. Cramb (Moray)
F.G. Mathers (Moray)
I.G. Taylor (Elgin)
M. Wilson (Moray)
C.J. Macleod (Moray)
R.M. Grant (Aberdeen Caledonian)
N.S. Grant (Moray)
C.J. Macleod (Moray)
J. McCallum (Moray)
N.S. Grant (Moray)
R.D. Morrison (Moray)
N. Robson (Elgin)
K. Hird (Murcar)
M.R. Ballantyne (Moray)
W. Bryce (East Kilbryde)
R.J. Sheils (Moray)
A. Junor (Forres)
A. Junor (Royal Dornoch)
A.J. Duncan (Moray)
D. Main (Moray)
N.S. Grant (Moray)
N.S. Grant (Moray)
S. Leith (Moray)
G. Thomson (Moray)
D. Baker (Crewe)
K. Thomson (Moray)
G. Thomson (Moray)
G. Thomson (Moray)

Handicap Section 1 – Macpherson Rose Bowl

— WINNERS —

1950	A. Willox		1978	S. Mitchell
1951	P. Stewart		1979	D.M. Rattray
1952	G.D. Kellas		1980	A.M. Farquhar
1953	W. Cowie		1981	I. MacDonald
1954	A. Morrison		1982	G.W. Cowper
1955	G.C. McKenzie		1983	W.E. MacLeman
1956	J.D. MacDonald		1984	A.J. Smith
1957	W. Simpson		1985	K.S. Wares
1958	A. Grant		1986	D.C. Smith
1959	A.R. Cairns		1987	R. Wilson
1960	J.G. Phimister		1988	J.W. Souter
1961	P.F. Smith		1989	K.M. Duncan
1962	W. Dean		1990	D.J.C. Cameron
1963	J.G. Phimister		1991	T. Mackie
1964	R.H. Allison		1992	W.M. Macleod
1965	R.A. Young		1993	N. Stewart
1966	D.G. Dempster		1994	J.W. Souter
1967			1995	J.R. McLeod
1968	B.W. Wilken		1996	D.M. Rattray
1969	J.D. Anderson		1997	P.H. Paton
1970	N.G. MacFarlane		1998	M. Richford
1971	D. Baillie		1999	G. Devine
1972	J.M. Duggie		2000	M. Cowie
1973	A.M. Farquhar		2001	M.R. Hamblin
1974	R. Sandison		2002	M. Dean
1975	D.J. Baillie		2003	P. Smith
1976	J.M. Duggie		2004	R. Tewnion
1977	A.A. McKenzie		2005	

Handicap Section 2 – Ross Anderson Trophy

WINNERS

1968	R.S. Phimister	1987	M.J. Sharp
1969	S. Willox	1988	A.R.C. Laing
1970	J.G. Robertson	1989	I. McNeill
1971	C. Terris	1990	S. Simpson
1972	R. Rothnie	1991	P.R. Wood
1973	C. Terris	1992	J.C. Grant
1974	G.E. Webb	1993	C. Forster
1975	M.M. MacLeman	1994	J. Dempster
1976	P. Thomson	1995	D.J.S. Main
1977	S. Stephen	1996	A. McDonald
1978	K.T. Rattray	1997	M. Laing
1979	P. McKendrick	1998	C. Sandison
1980	G. Millar	1999	J. Cordiner
1981	K. Raine	2000	W.A. Watson
1982	E.B. Souter	2001	B. Cross
1983	A. Flynn	2002	N. Cowper
1984	P. McKendrick	2003	S. Robertson
1985	G. Meldrum	2004	M. Underwood
1986	G.A. Muir	2005	

BIBLIOGRAPHY

Golfiana. A poem by George Fullerton Carnegie. (c.1833)

Between Two Wars. Bernard Darwin. (Chatto & Windus 1944)

Teach Yourself Golf. J.C. Jessop. (London 1950)

Golf at The Gallop. George Duncan (London 1951)

The Bobby Jones Story. Keeler and Rice (The Fireside Press 1955)

Knave of Clubs. Eric Brown. (London 1961)

Only on Sundays. Henry Longhurst (Cassell 1964)

Spinners Yarn. I.A.R. Peebles. (London 1977)

Personal Memories of Royal Dornoch Golf Club. Donald Grant (1978)

Golf in the Making. I.T. Henderson and D.I. Stirk. (Crawley 1979)

Royal Aberdeen Golf Club - 200 Years of Golf. J.A.G. Mearns (Aberdeen 1980)

The Moray Golf Club at Lossiemouth. John McConachie. (Moravian Press, Elgin 1988)

Sir Iain Tennant, K.T., of Innes House. Personal communication. (1989)

Aberdeen Press & Journal. (March 1989)

The Scottish Golf Guide 2nd Edition. David Hamilton. Canongate Books Ltd. (1995)

Golf – Scotland's Game. David Hamilton at The Partick Press (1998)

INDEX